SAMUEL NORVELL LAPSLEY.

Presbyterian Pioneers in Congo

BY

WILLIAM H. SHEPPARD

INTRODUCTION

BY

REV. S. H. CHESTER, D. D.

PUBLISHED BY

PRESBYTERIAN COMMITTEE OF PUBLICATION

RICHMOND, VA.

RICHMOND PRESS, INC.

PRINTERS

RICHMOND, VA.

To

THE SOUTHERN PRESBYTERIAN CHURCH

*Which took me as a half-clad, barefoot boy and trained me for the
ministry of Christ, and to which I owe all I
am or ever hope to be*

This Book is Gratefully Dedicated

by

THE AUTHOR

Contents

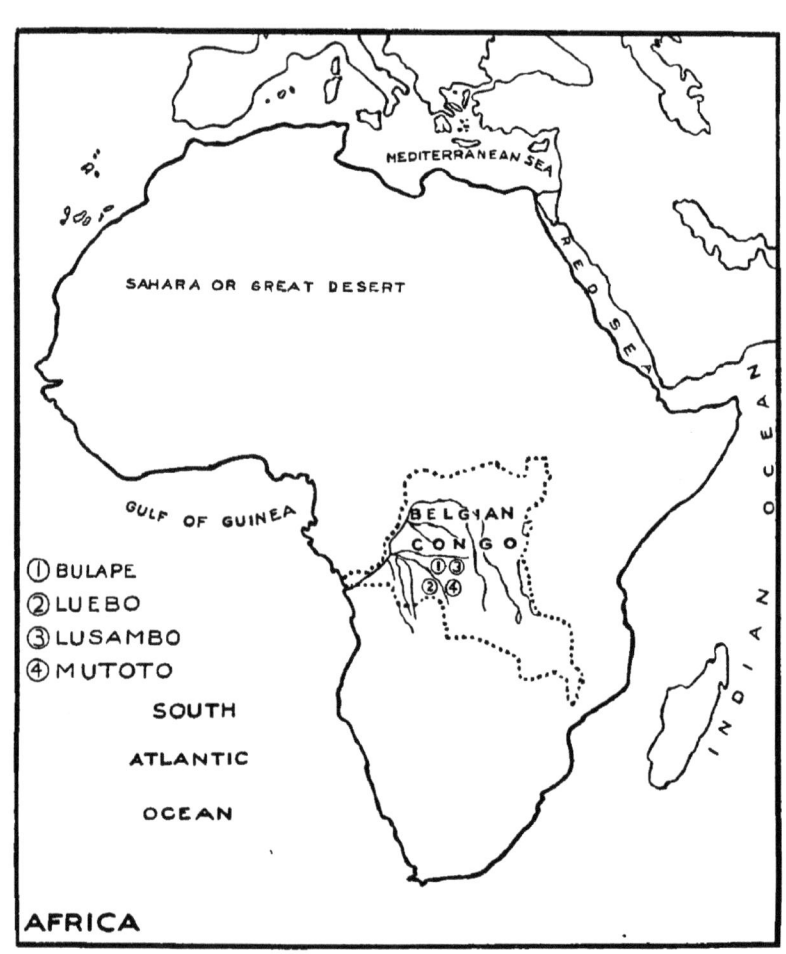

MEDITERRANEAN SEA

RED SEA

SAHARA OR GREAT DESERT

GULF OF GUINEA

BELGIAN
CONGO

① BULAPE
② LUEBO
③ LUSAMBO
④ MUTOTO

SOUTH

ATLANTIC

OCEAN

INDIAN OCEAN

AFRICA

Illustrations

WM. H. SHEPPARD AND MRS. SHEPPARD

Introduction

"PRESBYTERIAN PIONEERS IN CONGO" is an expansion of autobiographical and historical lectures delivered by its author, Rev. Wm. H. Sheppard, D. D., before hundreds of our Southern Presbyterian congregations and before a number of prominent churches in the North, and always listened to with profit and delight. On one occasion when called upon to introduce Dr. Sheppard in one of our congregations, I used these words:

"It is my privilege to introduce to you to-day perhaps the most distinguished and certainly the most widely known minister of our Southern Presbyterian Church. For one thing, he is the only minister on our roll holding a fellowship in the Royal Geographical Society of London. On behalf of the Executive Committee of Foreign Missions, I wish to say that there is no missionary on our roll more beloved or more highly esteemed by the Committee under which he serves. During the time of his missionary service he has been called to represent us on many important occasions. He has stood before kings, both white kings and black kings, as our representative. He has never represented us anywhere that we have not had reason to be proud of the manner in which he has done it. He is now recognized both in London and Brussels as one of the greatest of African missionaries. That for which the Committee of Foreign Missions esteems him most is not the fact that he has achieved this prominence and recognition, but that, having achieved it, he has come back to us the same simple-hearted, humble, earnest Christian man that he was when we first sent him out."

Dr. Sheppard went out as the companion of Rev. Samuel N. Lapsley, our first missionary martyr in the Congo. The reader will be struck with the way in which, in telling his story up to the time of Mr. Lapsley's death, he always keeps Mr. Lapsley to the front and himself in the background. At the same time he will observe, what Mr. Lapsley would be quick to acknowledge if he were living, that in many of the critical situations that arose it was the ready mother wit of the author of this book by means of which they were extricated. The characteristic modesty of Dr. Sheppard should not be permitted to deprive him of the honor which justly belongs to him as one of the two pioneers and founders of this Mission, which has developed into one of the most interesting and successful Missions to be found anywhere in the world. The story of its early days could scarcely be told in a more interesting manner than it is told in this volume.

On September 15, 1912, Dr. W. H. Sheppard was installed pastor of the Hancock Street Presbyterian Church in Louisville, Ky., one of the branches of the work of which the Rev. John Little is superintendent. He writes of Dr. Sheppard and his work during the past four and a half years as follows:

"He has given himself to this work in the same earnest and self-denying spirit that characterized his service in the Congo and has won the love and confidence of his associates and of the people among whom he labors. He has not only done much to build up the membership and train it properly, but he has also cultivated a friendly co-operative spirit with the other previously hostile denominations. After these years of association with him, we have come to feel that your estimate of him as expressed above is not exaggerated."

S. H. CHESTER.

WM. H. SHEPPARD, THE AUTHOR'S FATHER.
FANNIE SHEPPARD, THE AUTHOR'S MOTHER.

Presbyterian Pioneers in Congo

CHAPTER I.

A TEN THOUSAND MILE JOURNEY.

Many requests have been made of me to write something of my life. May I say that, even from the beginning, it has been a very checkered one. I shall dwell but lightly upon my American life of twenty-five years; speaking more in detail of my African life of twenty years.

I was born in Waynesboro, Virginia, a small town on the Chesapeake and Ohio Railroad. My parents, William and Fannie Sheppard (still living) are good Presbyterians. There are so many lovely traits about my parents I am puzzled which to mention. However, my father not only had family prayers, but my dear mother in putting me to bed would kneel and pray aloud with me rather than have me say alone, "Now I lay me down to sleep," etc. Mother would scratch my back (which I enjoyed very much), then put me snugly to bed, and in a few minutes I was asleep. Mother never turned anyone from her door who came begging, whether white or colored, without offering them such as she had. My father for many years was sexton of the First Presbyterian Church in our town.

The white people were always very kind to us—as they were to all the colored people.

My First Impression on the Subject of Being a Missionary.—While still a barefoot boy a beautiful Christian lady, Mrs. Ann Bruce, said to me one day,

"William, I pray for you, and hope some day you may go to Africa as a missionary."

I had never heard of Africa, and those words made a lasting impression. God bless that good lady, so interested in me and Africa.

My first work as a boy was carrying water from a pump a block away morning and evening for Mrs. Annie M. Lowry. This was during the summer months. My mother was then, and is to-day, bath maid at the Warm Springs, Virginia, and my father is still in the barber business. My sister Eva, older than I, had gone to Staunton, twelve miles from Waynesboro, to live with an aunt. With permission from my parents I soon joined her. After being there for some months, I heard of a family who wanted to hire a boy to look after a horse. I applied and secured the position, spending two years with Dr. S. H. Henkel (the dentist). In a back room of the doctor's office was a box filled with teeth. It puzzled me much to think how in the world the people on resurrection day were to get their own teeth back. I loved my new home, for Dr. Henkel and his wife were so kind to me. They spent much time in instructing me in my books at night.

My next work was waiting in the McCurdy House at Clifton Forge, Va. Later I was sent to Covington, Va., also a McCurdy House, as head waiter. This was a promotion, though there were only two of us as waiters in the house. While at Covington I heard of the Hampton Normal and Industrial Institute. I secured some literature from there and read carefully every word. I saved my money, and in 1880 said good-bye to my parents and was off for school. I had made no formal application, but good General Armstrong, President of the Institute, received me kindly. The first year I worked on the farm, and later worked in the bakery, going to school at night. I loved to swim and fish, and every advantage was afforded me. The Hampton creek was filled with fish, oysters and crabs, and the broad ocean beyond was at my disposal.

General Armstrong was my ideal of manhood: his erect carriage, deep, penetrating eyes, pleasant smiles and kindly disposition drew all students to him. He was a great, tender-hearted father to us all, and the teachers were also deeply interested in the welfare of the students.

Dr. H. B. Frissell, who was chaplain of the Institute, was also a loving, congenial friend to us all. One Sabbath afternoon he asked me to accompany him and some of the teachers to establish a mission Sunday-school at Slabtown, a small village of poor colored people about a mile from the school. I went with him gladly and carried some of the Bibles and hymn books. I felt from that afternoon that my future work was to carry the gospel to the poor, destitute and forgotten people. Dr. Frissell, God bless him, was one of the humblest and most consecrated Christian gentlemen I ever knew.

From Hampton I returned to my parents' home in Waynesboro. Then I applied to our Church to be taken under the care of the Presbytery, and to be sent to the Theological Institute at Tuscaloosa, Ala.

Our dear good pastor, Rev. Frank McCutchan, who was deeply interested in me, wrote Dr. Stillman, the founder and President of the Institute, a letter concerning me. A reply soon came that I would be accepted. I humbly bowed my head in grateful thanks to Him who has said, "Whatsoever ye shall ask in prayer, believing, ye shall receive."

At Tuscaloosa Theological Institute.—A question asked me in my examination by both the Presbytery in Waynesboro, Va., and by the faculty of the Tuscaloosa Institute was: "If you are called upon to go to Africa as a missionary, would you be willing to go?" I promptly answered, "I would go, and with pleasure."

During my three years in the Institute I did missionary work around the town, visiting and praying with the sick—a work which I enjoyed so much.

Dr. Stillman longed to do something for the uplift of the colored ministry. The white citizens co-operated heartily with him in this mission of love. Some of our most prominent white ladies taught in the colored Sunday-school organized by the Church.

From Tuscaloosa I was called to take charge of a church in Montgomery, Ala. Three years were spent here very profitably, as I believe.

I was called to Atlanta, Ga., and was ordained pastor of the Harrison Street Presbyterian Church in 1887. For a number of years I applied to our Foreign Mission Board, whose headquarters were then in Baltimore. My appeals met with no success then, but I was not discouraged. I made a trip to our Foreign Mission office and laid my plans before our secretary, Dr. M. H. Houston.

In 1890 the joyful tidings came that Rev. S. N. Lapsley, a young white man of Anniston, Ala., and I had been appointed as missionaries of the Southern Presbyterian Church to Africa, and that we were to proceed to the Congo Independent State, West Central Africa, as soon as we could prepare for the journey. My heart had never been made so happy. Rev. Mr. Lapsley and I met the Executive Committee in Nashville, Tenn. Many questions were asked us about the new country to which we were going. Mr. Lapsley was intelligent on many of the questions asked; I knew a few things which I had learned from geography, but it was all very vague. We decided to meet in New York and sail from that port to England.

Setting Sail for England.—In 1890, as the *Adriatic* slowly steamed out from the pier in New York City, a kind lady called out as she waved, "Sheppard, take care of Sam." It was Mrs. Lapsley, wife of Judge James W. Lapsley, of Alabama. This good lady had given her prayers and money to the Master for the cause of Foreign Missions and now she gave of her own flesh and blood her son, and waved him a sad farewell.

Judge Lapsley and his wife returned to their home in Alabama—that home had changed, there was a vacant chair and a voice that was not heard. Our faces were turned now toward Africa, next to the largest continent of the world, the richest, the darkest, and the most neglected.

It is sad to leave home, friends and native land and seek a home among strangers, yet it was for the Master's sake.

> "Native land, we love thee;
> All thy scenes, we love them well;
> Home, and friends which smile around us,
> Can we leave thee? Can we say farewell?
> Far in heathen lands to dwell?
>
> "Yes, we hasten from thee gladly
> To the strangers, let us tell
> How He died, the Blessed Saviour,
> To redeem a world from hell—
> Native land, Farewell, farewell!"

The *Adriatic* soon put a vast space between us and our home people like a blank page in existence.

During the voyage of eleven days which brought us to Liverpool, we had the pleasure of seeing whales, porpoises, and flying fish. From Liverpool we went by rail to London, where we received the greatest hospitality possible at "Harley House" from Dr. Grattan Guinness and family. They spared no pains in helping us in every way they could. We hadn't words to express our gratitude to them. This whole family was imbued with the missionary spirit.

Securing Our African Supplies.—After exchanging most of our American money for cowrie shells, beads, salt and brass wire—these were our future currency—we purchased flour, sugar, butter and lard; also thin linen clothing and helmets for the sun.

While our outfit and supplies were being gotten together, we made ourselves useful in accepting invitations to speak and in visiting places of interest. Some of the places where we spoke were Hyde Park, Burger Hall, East London Tabernacle, Hary House, Edinbourgh Castle, Dr. Barmandos Orphanage, and White Chapel. We visited the Bank of England, Crystal Palace, Tower of London, Houses of Parliament, Westminster Abbey, Royal Exchange, British Museum, St. Paul's Cathedral, and Livingstone's grave. The sightseeing helped in our business affairs and we were made exceedingly comfortable in a strange land and city by Mr. Robert Whyte, of 51 King Henry's Road, a splendid Christian gentleman.

From London to Rotterdam.—At the Liverpool Street Railroad station a number of friends had gathered. They sang gospel hymns as our train pulled out for Harwich. The train was soon well under way, speeding along the ringing rails at a mile a minute till we reached Harwich. Here we went aboard a steamer, which puffed and ploughed through the heavy sea all night and landed us in Rotterdam, Holland, early next morning. Were we sea sick? Well, we lost in this single night all the flesh which we had gained in our long stay in England. There is no sickness, to me, like sea-sickness. It is a combination of all maladies.

Toward evening we boarded the *Afrikaan*, a small Dutch trading ship, bound for the Congo. The other passengers were English and Swedish missionaries and Dutch traders. We had a good supply of a cure for sea-sickness, but when we were well out where the wind blew we found that meals and medicine forsook us.

Arrival at Banana—"Sharks Point."—After nearly three weeks sailing we sighted "Sharks Point" on the great Congo river.

We disembarked here, our first stop in the Dark Continent. The beach was thronged with half-clad natives, called Luongas. We found this point well named, for the river swarmed with man-eating sharks.

Our First Excitement. While bathing in the surf one afternoon, Mr. Lapsley called in a loud, distressing voice as he rushed out on the beach and lay speechless for a moment. Coming near him he exclaimed, "I was nearly taken by a shark."

The Congo river at this point by actual measurement is seven miles wide. If you include the sand banks, small streams and pools, it is seventeen miles wide, and the dark, tea-colored water can be discerned one hundred and fifty miles out at sea. There are thousands of banana trees growing on the narrow peninsula.

Our first dinner on shore at a trading post was enjoyed very much. We ate bananas until we were embarrassed. When we went out on the shady side of the house we beckoned to the native who had been waiting on the table and made him understand that we were from a country where bananas were scarce, and that we wanted him to bring us a few more, if it was convenient to him. The fellow smiled and bowed, showing that he understood us, and in a few minutes he came back with as many bananas as he could carry.

A Start for Boma.—Our next stop was at Boma, the capital of the Congo Free State. The name means "Python." The principal part of the town is on the slope of a hill. Near the river it is swampy and in the marshes the alligator and boa-constrictor make their home.

A Joke on Us.—On board ship we usually had for dinner soup, roast beef, vegetables and dessert. At Boma we went into a Portuguese hotel to take dinner. Being very hungry, we had soup twice, a good helping of fish followed, then came beef and vegetables. Thinking this was all, we ate like wild men. Our plates were taken away and soon a new course was brought in. We refused. (Had to.) Pretty soon another course. Others at the table who had eaten more moderately and knew there were six more courses smiled at us every time fresh plates were brought. And there we sat, certainly an hour, and very uncomfortable, until dessert was served. There were perhaps about seventy foreigners in Boma —Belgians, Portuguese and English.

Steaming for Matadi.—After a short stay in Boma we continued on our river journey to Matadi, one hundred and eighty miles from the sea. Matadi is a native name, meaning stones.

We mentioned to a missionary that the natives were very active and swift. The missionary explained that if we had those stones under our bare feet we would move, too. The sun seems to shine nowhere so hot as down upon these slick stones. We found about fifteen foreigners here, most of them Belgians and Dutch. They were very yellow from the effects of the sun and fever.

MATADI AND THE CONGO RIVER.

CHAPTER II.

MATADI AND STANLEY POOL.

Introduction to an African Fever—In speaking of fever, we made the acquaintance of three forms of African fever; remittent, intermittent, and bilious hermaturic. They are not contagious, but a mosquito which has bitten an infected person inoculates that poison into your blood and causes the fever.

Mr. Lapsley and I both had fever at the same time with about the same rise of temperature and duration. The kind missionaries of the Baptist Mission, Messrs. Lawson Forfeitt, and S. C. Graham, gave us five grains of calomel and five grains of jalap each, and told us to go to bed. We were covered with six blankets, hot tea, cup after cup, followed in quick succession, and soon we were like two ducks in a puddle of water. We had never perspired so in all our days. The Missionaries were kept busy from room to room keeping the blankets on us. On a day when it was 99 in the shade and not possible to register in the sun, we were under six blankets, and on the outside of all that calomel, jalap tea, and fifty grains of quinine. It was enough to kill the fever, which it did effectually.

Our First Hunt.—We were anxious to try our guns, and in company with two natives, we went down the river about a mile, shot an enormous eagle, a black monkey and a water snake seven feet long. The natives were delighted with the eagle and the monkey for their supper but threw the snake away. The natives told us that there were plenty of buffalo about two miles away in the deep grass, but we made ourselves contented with the game we had and returned to the mission station.

In Hell's Cauldron.—The waters of the great Congo river and its hundreds of tributaries, as with the rush of a mighty mill race, make an acute turn just here, and form a deep, dashing, dangerous whirl-pool. Only the strongest ocean steamers can breast the current, with safety. The people told us of a Portuguese steamer which was swallowed up trying to make her way through the pool.

The moaning of the seething sea-serpent, can be heard a mile away. Being ignorant of its great drawing power, we tried to cross the river, three hundred yards above. In spite of our desperate efforts to reach the north bank we were drawn in as a floating stick. We spun round and round like a top, the boat all the time at an angle of about forty degrees, till we were dizzy. Natives on shore informed the other missionaries of our perilous predicament. We thought of our watery graves and all of our past life flashed before us. "Oh! save us Master, or we perish," we prayed. In a moment, as if miraculously, the seething cauldron ceased for a second, and by an awful struggle for life, we rowed out and landed, to the delight of the excited crowd.

Mounds of Triumphant Martyrs.—Down at the bottom of the hill near the river bank shaded by evergreens is the sacred spot. Faithful missionaries of Jesus are sleeping there.

In Great Britain, Sweden, and America they were told that the climate was deadly; that they would be pelted by the rains, scorched by the sun, and murdered by the natives. Yet in full knowledge of these conditions and with hearts imbued with the spirit of God they went forth on their mission of love. A kiss upon the cheek, a mingling of tears, a wave of the handkerchief and they were off on their errand for their King.

Emaciated by deadly fevers, pelted by tropical storms, stung by the tsetse flies fresh from the lazarette of misery, fatigued and foot sore from many a tramp, they have laid themselves down in this pleasant dale "Till He comes."

Our Tramp to Stanley Pool.—Africa is divided into the following races: the Vardens occupying the North, the Fulah in the Soudan, the Bantu in Central Africa, the Hottentot and the Kaffirs in the South. These races are divided into 683 tribes, and as they differ in name so they differ in habits, customs and conditions.

The navigable part of the Congo river from the Atlantic ocean ends here under the Livingstone Cataracts, but above the 250 miles of succession of cataracts we are told that the great Congo is navigable for a thousand miles. There are no wagons, horses, camels or oxen in this region. The Ba-Congo native is the burden bearer. There are 40,000 on the caravan road of 250 miles between Matadi and Stanley Pool. These men go up bearing loads of beads, brass wire, bales of cloth, cowrie shells and European provisions of all kinds. The carriers on their return journey to Matadi bring ivory, rubber, cam wood and gum copal. The carrying capacity of each native's head is sixty-five pounds.

On the 27th of June, 1890, we secured twenty-five of these burden-bearers to carry our loads of tent, beds, bedding, trunks, chairs, guns, corned beef, hard tack, lard, salt, tea, coffee and sugar. We wrote carefully in our memorandums the name and town of each man, for we were told that very often a carrier hearing of the death of some relative will leave the caravan without notifying you, and the period of mourning often lasts six months.

It has been known that sometimes traders coming into camp in the evening would find that their food, cooking utensils, tent or something very necessary was five or six miles off in some other village. Having the name and town of your missing man, you can send runners to bring back your needed load.

Saying good-bye to the kind missionaries, we started out at the rear of our Indian filing caravan on a trail about twelve inches broad and running as crooked as a snake down and up hill, over rough stones, and through high grass. After three hours hard marching we came to our first river, the Mpozo. The river was not very deep or broad, but it was clear and swift and one solid bed of boulders. A few calls from our head man brought the boatman from his shack, and he soon had us ferried across in a native canoe.

Our First Congo Tramp.—By the help of the natives we soon had our tent stretched, the ground sheet spread inside, and the couches made up. One of the natives brought us an armful of wood and the camp fire was started. We asked the head man if any of the caravan knew how to cook, and the response was, "They all know how to cook." We were told that all men belonging to the caravan learned to cook. A cook demands extra pay and also gets fat "en route" by tasting the food.

We had for our first supper crackers, jam, tea and river water.

Mountain Climbing.—We were up at five o'clock, had breakfast, an exact duplicate of our supper, and began to climb over stones, around cliffs, following the narrow trail for three hours till we reached the top, footsore and hungry.

Near the top of this mountain there is a mission of the American Baptist Union, which bears the name of the mountain, Mpalabala. We were received most cordially by all the missionaries and were soon rested on a cool veranda. We were shown around the Mission compound, the chapel, the school, the dispensary, and the native town which was near by. We also heard some good singing in the native tongue.

In the afternoon we started our downward trail, slipping and sliding over sharp rocks and slippery boulders, till we reached a creek at the bottom. Having learned how, we had less trouble getting up the tent here than we had at the Mpozo. We had for our supper corned beef, crackers, tea and creek water.

The missionaries told us to begin our marches about five o'clock A. M. and rest in some shady place by a stream from eleven until four, march again for two hours, and camp, thus making eight hours a day, or about twenty-five miles in the eight hours.

Where Stanley Passed.—The country just this side of the mountain is not so hilly or rocky as that near Matadi. We found a road had been made by Mr. Stanley and saw some of Stanley's heavy iron wagon wheels lying by the roadside; also sun-bleached skeletons of native carriers here and there who by sickness, hunger or fatigue, had laid themselves down to die, without fellow or friend.

A Warning to Others.—We passed an old market place on the plain and near by a palm tree were two old flint-lock muskets driven into the ground, muzzle first. It was explained to us that for murder two men had been tried, condemned, and hung in the public market.

Their bodies had been eaten by leopards and jackals and their guns driven into the ground as a visible warning to others.

Sick and Helpless and Ready to Die.—In passing a cluster of bushes we heard groans of a native, and on making our way into the thicket found a man dying of smallpox. We longed to help him, but there was nothing we could do, and our head man hurried us away, fearing we ourselves might catch the disease.

Nearing the A. B. M. U.—The fifth day of our tramp brought us to M'Banza Manteka, a mission station of the American Baptist Union. How glad we were to see foreigners again. We were received kindly by the missionaries, who asked for American news and told us many profitable things about Congo, its customs, climate, etc., and how they had with great difficulty and danger built the station; how they learned the native language, translated hymns and the Scriptures; of their elephant hunts and leopard scares; and how a big leopard with a hog in his mouth had jumped a six-foot pen. They talked of trials and triumphs till the night was far spent.

In the morning we had the pleasure of seeing a neat, large galvanized iron church. This building was given by Dr. Gordon's Church of Boston, Mass., and shipped to Africa in sections. The Christians of the neighborhood banded themselves together *en masse*, walked five days' journey to Matadi, and on their heads and shoulders through the rocky trail brought 237 loads, equal to six tons, which would have cost the mission $1,000.00. The Christian women who could not go paid men to bring up their part. Some of the women who had but little money gathered their garden stuff, accompanied the men, feeding and cheering them on their way.

The church here has 400 Christian men and women, and we are told that they preach the Lord Jesus Christ beautifully in their lives.

We saw the collection baskets, one at the entrance of each door. They were the size of big clothes baskets. The missionaries told us that every Sunday these baskets are filled by the Christians with strings of blue beads, their money. .

Our First Congo Service.—The missionaries had supplied us with a "Ki-Kongo" Testament and a native hymn book. We pitched our tent near a beautiful cool stream. At nine o'clock the dish pan (bell) was beaten and the caravan assembled for divine service. Dr. Lapsley read Luke 2:1, 2 and we sang "We're Marching to Zion." One of our carriers offered prayer, then Mr. Lapsley and I followed in prayer in English. The natives sang splendidly and heartily.

Off for Lukunga.—At daybreak Monday morning we had finished our breakfast by candle light and with staff in hand we marched northeast for Lukunga.

In two days we sighted the Mission Compound. Word had reached the missionaries (A. B. M. U.) that foreigners were approaching, and they came out to meet and greet us. We were soon hurried into their cool and comfortable mud houses. Our faithful cook was dismissed, for we were to take our meals with the missionaries.

Scorpions and Spiders.—Mr. Hoste, who is at the head of this station, came into our room and mentioned that the numerous spiders, half the size of your hand, on the walls were harmless. "But," said he as he raised his hand and pointed to a hole over the door, "there is a nest of scorpions; you must be careful in moving in and out, for they will spring upon you."

Well, you ought to have seen us dodging in and out that door. After supper, not discrediting the veracity of the gentleman, we set to work, and for an hour we spoiled the walls by smashing spiders with slippers.

A Big Boa.—The next morning the mission station was excited over the loss of their only donkey. The donkey had been feeding in the field and a boa-constrictor had captured him, squeezed him into pulp, dragged him a hundred yards down to the river bank, and was preparing to swallow him. The missionaries, all with guns, took aim and fired, killing the twenty-five-foot boa-constrictor. The boa was turned over to the natives and they had a great feast. The missionaries told us many tales about how the boa-constrictor would come by night and steal away their goats, hogs and dogs.

Miniature Fleas.—The sand around Lukunga is a hot-bed for miniature fleas, or "jiggers." The second day of our stay at Lukunga our feet had swollen and itched terribly, and on examination we found that these "jiggers" had entered under our toe nails and had grown to the size of a pea. A native was called and with a small sharpened stick they were cut out. We saw natives with toes and fingers eaten entirely off by these pests. Mr. Hoste told us to keep our toes well greased with palm oil. We followed his instructions, but grease with sand and sun made our socks rather "heavy."

A Live Church.—The native church here is very strong spiritually. The church bell, a real big brass bell, begins to ring at 8 A. M. and continues for an hour. The natives in the neighborhood come teeming by every trail, take their seats quietly, and listen attentively to the preaching of God's word. No excitement, no shouting, but an intelligent interest shown by looking and listening from start to finish.

In the evening you can hear from every quarter our hymns sung by the natives in their language. They are having their family devotions before retiring.

We are told that many evangelists had been educated on the spot and sent out into the country to tell their brothers the story of Jesus and his love.

Off for Stanley Pool.—After a very pleasant and profitable stay at Lukunga we continued our march toward Stanley Pool. Our cook smiled—he was reinstated.

"Crocks" in the N'Kissy.—Our second day's march brought us to a large river. Our loads and men were ferried over in canoes. Mr. Lapsley and I decided to swim it, and so we jumped in and struck out for the opposite shore. On landing we were told by a native watchman that we had done a very daring thing. He explained with much excitement and many gestures that the river was filled with crocodiles, and that he did not expect to see us land alive on his side. We camped on the top of the hill overlooking N'Kissy and the wild, rushing Congo Rapids. It was in one of these whirlpools that young Pocock, Stanley's last survivor, perished.

A Native Market.—The next day we were up and off at an early hour. After about ten hours' march we saw in the distance a great number of people and heard their loud talking. We were told that it was a native market. We had already noticed that our men had an extra move on them. We arrived in the market and took shelter under a large tree. Our men soon put down their loads and joined in the noisy crowd. In a little while we lost sight of our carriers, for all the market men looked alike to us.

A number of women had their faces, hair and loin

cloths smeared over with a black preparation which trickled all down their legs. On inquiry we were told that it was a tar made from burned peanuts, palm oil and palm nuts. It was their mode of mourning for the deceased. The babies which were tied to their backs and exposed to the hot sun were well tarred also. There were hogs, dogs, ducks, goats, sheep, rats, bats, chickens and caterpillars in numbers and abundance. Monkeys, parrots, peanuts, beans, fresh and dried, fish, pineapples, bananas, clay pots and pipes for sale. We saw piles of native bread made from the roots of manioc. This bread was round like a man's head, wrapped in greased banana leaves, weighing about five pounds. In appearance and eating it is like putty.

It was impossible to get our carriers together, and so we were compelled to camp at the market place for the night, and such eating! They had turned the whole plateau into a cooking plant. Our men being well supplied with food made splendid marches the last two days.

Arriving at Stanley Pool.—A broad road led to the entrance of the settlement. The missionaries being notified came on the way and welcomed us to their African homes.

We met Dr. Aaron Sims and Mr. Reign, of the American Baptist Union; Rev. Roger and Rev. Gordon, of the English Baptist Missionary Society; Rev. and Mrs. McKittrick, of the Congo Bololo Mission; and Dr. Harrison, of the American Methodist Mission.

The Pool.—As we sat in the mission house there was a beautiful expanse of water before us (Stanley Pool), twenty-five miles long and about nine miles broad, dotted here and there with large, grassy islands.

Within a hundred yards of the mission station was

also a native village, the Bateke people, of a thousand inhabitants. The Bateke is a tribe of the Bantu race, tall, slight, and apparently not very strong. Their chief occupation is trading. The up-river people, who are great elephant hunters, come in big canoes to Stanley Pool with ivory, gum, copal and cam wood. They sell to the Bateke people, and in turn the Bateke traded to foreigners living near the coast.

The frame work of their houses is made of split bamboo with long dried grass tied on for roof and walls. They are about fifteen feet long and seven feet broad, oval shaped, and entered by a sliding door three feet high.

Visiting through the village, we were introduced to Chief N'Galiama, who entertained us by showing some of his presents given him by foreigners—china plates, cups, knives, spoons, hats, caps, beads, etc. He showed also a white handkerchief with W. M. Stanley's name on it. We asked the old chief to give it to us, but he refused; then we tried to buy it, but he would not part with the handkerchief of the great explorer. The religious work with these people was not very hopeful. They were reserved, hard to reach, and clung to their idols of wood.

Mr. Lapsley Leaves for Bolobo.—After eleven days stay at Stanley Pool, Mr. Lapsley left for Bolobo, a mission station of the Baptist Missionary Society, five days' steaming up the Congo river, to elicit information from Rev. George Grenfell, a missionary and explorer.

My First Hippopotamus.—In the "Pool" we saw many hippopotami, and longed to go out in a canoe and shoot one, but being warned of the danger from the hippopotami and also of the treacherous current of the Congo river, which might take us over the rapids and to death, we were afraid to venture. A native Bateke fisherman, just a few days before our arrival, had been crushed in his canoe by a bull-hippopotamus. Many stories of hippopotami horrors were told us.

One day Chief N'Galiama with his attendant came to the mission and told Dr. Simms that the people in the village were very hungry and to see if it were possible for him to get some meat to eat.

Dr. Simms called me and explained how the people were on the verge of a famine and if I could kill them a hippopotamus it would help greatly. He continued to explain that the meat and hide would be dried by the people and, using but a little at each meal, would last them a long time. Dr. Simms mentioned that he had never hunted, but he knew where the game was. He said, "I will give you a native guide, you go with him around the first cataract about two miles from here and you will find the hippopotami." I was delighted at the idea, and being anxious to use my "Marteni Henry" rifle and to help the hungry people, I consented to go. In an hour and a half we had walked around the rapids, across the big boulders, and right before us were at least a dozen big hippopotami. Some were frightened, ducked their heads and made off; others showed signs of fight and defiance.

At about fifty yards distant I raised my rifle and let fly at one of the exposed heads. My guide told me that the hippopotamus was shot and killed. In a few minutes another head appeared above the surface of the water and again taking aim I fired with the same result. The guide, who was a subject of the Chief N'Galiama, sprung upon a big boulder and cried to me to look at the big bubbles which were appearing on the water; then explained in detail that the hippopotami had drowned and would rise to the top of the water within an hour. The guide asked to go to a fishing camp nearby and call some men to secure the hippopotami when they rose, or else they would go out with the current and over the rapids. In a very short time about fifty men, bringing native rope with them, were on the scene and truly, as the guide had said, up came the first hippopotamus, his big back showing first. A number of the men were off swimming with the long rope which was tied to the hippopotamus' foot. A signal was given and every man did his best. No sooner had we secured the one near shore than there was a wild shout to untie and hasten for the other. These two were securely tied by their feet and big boulders were rolled on the rope to keep them from drifting out into the current.

The short tails of both of them were cut off and we started home. We reported to Dr. Simms that we had about four or five tons of meat down on the river bank. The native town ran wild with delight. Many natives came to examine my gun which had sent the big bullets crashing through the brain of the hippopotami. Early the next morning N'Galiama sent his son Nzelie with a long caravan of men to complete the work. They leaped upon the backs of the hippopotami, wrestled with each other for a while, and then with knives and axes fell to work. The missionaries enjoyed a hippopotamus steak that day also.

Hunting Hippopotami Around Stanley Pool.— Hunting, though a pleasant and profitable pastime and a splendid way in which to pick up the native language, is an exceedingly dangerous one. One day the Bateke natives came running all excited saying there was a big female hippo feeding on a small grassy island not five hundred yards from the Mission Compound. Dr.

Simms called out, "Get your gun, go quickly, there is a hippo on the island."

Six men were in readiness with paddles in hand and as soon as I had stepped in the canoe off they pulled at full speed. In a few minutes we were alongside the island under cover of the long grass. The wise hippo scented us and started for the water, but with the crack of my rifle she fell in her tracks, killed instantly. A great shout came from the crowd of men, women and children on the beach.

In an hour's time with a score of men the hippo had been cut up and transported to the main shore. More than a ton of meat was sold to the hundreds of natives and given to the chiefs.

Banqua's Spirit.—With two large canoes and fourteen men pulling against a current we were soon at a point sixteen miles from the mission. Our canoes were dragged up on the sand and the natives told me to follow them. We made our way with great difficulty through the high grass and reached a small lake in the center of the island. There were six hippopotami in the lake. One of them, a very large bull hippo, bowed his neck, grunted in a deep bass voice, and came rushing toward the bank. The natives quickly surrounded me, explaining that the spirit of one of the chiefs (named Banqua) dwelt in that hippo and not to shoot it. They said, "If that hippo is killed our chief will also die, and we will have plenty of trouble with our town when we return."

I gave attention to their superstition and waited for them to point out the proper one. In a few minutes the hippopotami reappeared on the surface of the water. The bull remained within ten yards of us, bellowing at the top of his voice. The natives pointed out a dark brown female about fifty yards away. I raised my rifle and the bullet entered the head of the hippo just under the ear, and she sank slowly and quietly to the bottom of the lake.

The natives soon had the grass cleared, a fire burning, and their sharp knives in readiness for a feast.

While waiting for our hippo to rise we waded through the grass and marsh a quarter of a mile, and there to our great surprise, not more than forty yards away, stood an elephant quietly grazing. We stopped and gazed at the monster. I thought of the quantity of meat which we had already secured, and retraced our steps to the lake. The natives were very much exercised over my not shooting the elephant. I told them it was not right to kill simply to be killing, and as we have no steamboat to carry the meat away, it would lie here in the sun and decay.

By this time our hippo had floated and I called to the men to take the rope, swim in and tie it to the nose and we would pull it near the shore. Not a man moved, though they were all good swimmers.

One of the men explained that the lake was filled with crocodiles.

I said to him, "You do not see a crocodile in the whole lake. You men are too timid, you are afraid of a dead hippo."

I pressed upon two of the men as strongly as possible to take the rope and swim away.

One of the natives politely asked if people in the foreign country could swim. "Yes," I replied, "and they are good swimmers, too; and if you won't go after that hippo, I will."

But another said, "Don't go, the wind will blow it to shore."

Taking the rope and putting the loop on my arm, I jumped in and swam to the hippo. As I began to tie the rope around her nose up came a monster crocodile and made a terrible lunge at her neck. Not a moment did I tarry to see what effect his sharp teeth had on the hippo, but turned the rope loose and under the water I went, and was half way to the shore when I came up. The natives were very much excited and assisted me in landing. I begged their pardon and was ashamed of my bravery.

Many times in Central Africa foreigners get into serious difficulties from which they cannot extricate themselves by disregarding the advice of natives.

Sure enough by 3 P. M. our hippo, having been blown by the gentle breeze, was lying alongside the shore. There were any number of crocodile heads in sight and several very near the hippo, sniffing the blood. After cutting off a good, substantial steak, we enjoyed a hearty supper and retired for the night under a beautiful moonlit sky.

At 6 o'clock in the morning we began cutting up our hippo and by 12 o'clock we were loaded and under way on our return journey. The men sang and paddled and were happy until the wind rose and the waves of the Congo threatened to swamp us. Then they began to call upon their idols to save them. We rounded "Gallina Point," one of the most dangerous places on the river, our canoes going at full speed with the strong current, and early the same afternoon we landed at the mission, disposed of our cargo, and sat down to think and talk of our adventure.

Through the Cataracts.—Before many days had elapsed, there was a call to shoot another hippopotamus which was about 600 yards direct out from the mission just above the first cataract.

In a few minutes the native men were ready. One canoe glided along swiftly, keeping the hippo to the left of us. It disappeared several times under the water, but at last, excited by our challenge, he started for the canoe, and within twenty yards of us he received the bullet in the forehead and down he sank. We returned to the beach and in an hour he rose to the surface of the water.

We were off again, the men plying their paddles with power. When the floating monster was reached, we succeeded in tying him by the nose with a short rope, which was also tied to the canoe.

All ready, we started with all our strength towing our cargo, but it was useless; the current was too strong and we had drifted too near the rapids.

I pulled a knife from my belt, cut the rope, and directed the men to turn the bow of the canoe towards the rapids. With strong arm and steady nerves those men guided the canoe through the dashing waves to a bay of safely below.

The hippo was found the next day washed upon the sand by a strong back current.

To the Rescue of Mr. Rogers.—I was· invited by Rev. Rogers to take another hunt with him for hippopotami in the Pool. Mr. Rogers with his canoe led the way. At noon we landed on a sandbank and prepared dinner from a wild duck shot on the way. After dinner it was suggested that we cross the Congo to the north bank. My canoe led the way. When half way across the river my men called out excitedly, "Hguva kuvanda Mundele!" (a hippo is killing the white man.) I called out, "Vutuka!" (Return), and in an instant my canoe was right about and under way. All the paddlers from Mr. Rogers' canoe had jumped out and were swimming toward shore. As the great brute rushed to crush the canoe I let fly, shooting him through the brain. We pulled alongside of the missionary's canoe and towed him into shore.

In an hour's time we had landed our hippo and were busy cutting him up. We returned the same afternoon to the mission.

Around Stanley Pool within a short time we had killed thirty-six hippopotami. The proceeds from these hunts we used toward helping to defray our expenses while we were delayed at Stanley Pool.

CHAPTER III.

THE KWANGO EXPEDITION.

Hunting Porters for the Kasai-Kwango Expedition.—Not being able to hire carriers at Stanley Pool, it was necessary to take a journey 140 miles into the cataract region to find men. I made the journey, secured twenty-five men, and returned to Stanley Pool.

Mr. Lapsley's Return from Bolobo.—I reached Stanley Pool on the 25th of October and found Mr. Lapsley in good health and fine spirits. He had enjoyed his up-river trip and received much help and information from the kind missionaries of the Baptist Missionary Society.

We had a talk with the twenty-five men about our plans to take an overland journey to Kinkunji. We told them that we were prospecting for a new Mission Society (The Southern Presbyterian). The men listened attentively, but when dawn broke there was not a man of them to be found. They had heard of the hostility of the Kwango people and so decided to return to their own homes.

Mr. Lapsley Gets a Fresh Set of Men.—On October 28th Mr. Lapsley started down country in search of fresh men for our Kinkunji journey. By December 3rd he had collected the necessary men and returned to us at Stanley Pool.

Decide on River Journey.—We had prayer for the Master's guidance, and after talking over our plans thoroughly we decided to take our journey by water and not overland.

Renting a Canoe.—For our journey a canoe was needed, and I was detailed to hire a large one from N'Guba, a Bateke chief. I succeeded in getting a large, strong canoe by promising its return with not less than a hundred pounds of dried hippo meat as pay.

Ready for the Journey.—On December 11th our canoe was lashed alongside the S. S. Henry Reed. Mr. Billington, an A. M. B. U. missionary and captain of the steamer, kindly consented to tow us on our journey as far as he went.

In the canoe was placed our tent, camp beds, cooking utensils, some clothing, our guns, and barter goods of white domestic, beads and brass wire. At the bow of the canoe we tied "Tippotib," a black Stanley Falls monkey. In a few hours Stanley Pool with its white-washed Mission Compound was left far behind us.

We Purchase a Big Canoe.—On December 16th we put into a village near the confluence of the Kasai with the Congo river. The villagers, Bayansie, were not hostile, but received us kindly. We saw a beautiful canoe which could easily hold fifteen or more paddlers. We needed *that* canoe, and in less than an hour's time we had bought it and hired more men for our river journey.

Farewell to the S. S. Henry Reed.—Saying good-bye to the missionaries, we started on our journey via the Kasai river. The men had a stiff pull in the strong current when turning out of the Congo into the Kasai.

Christmas in Central Africa.—December 25, 1891. Christmas morning we started early on our journey. Crossing to the left bank, where a number of canoes were moored under some shade trees, we discovered a trail. Making our canoe fast, we followed the trail through the forest and came upon a fortified village.

After much parley with the villagers the gate was opened and we entered. We were glad to buy fresh buffalo meat and eggs, giving in exchange beads. We then returned to our canoes. During the day a guinea fowl, an eagle, and a very large red monkey were killed. At nightfall we camped near a village. The people were friendly and were much interested in the preparation of our feast of eagle fowl and monkey.

After supper we had our usual nightly devotions, the crew and villagers being present.

Mr. Lapsley's Big Hippo.—The following day Mr. Lapsley shot a wild pigeon, a duck and a hippopotamus, and the whole night was spent in drying hippo meat over a big fire.

The First Sermon in the Kasai.—December 28th being Sunday, we spent it quietly in the forest near the river bank. Mr. Lapsley had charge of the services. His was the first known sermon ever preached and the first hymn ever sung in that great Kasai valley.

Welcome by Queen N'Gankabe.—On Monday we made a good run. In the afternoon Mr. Lapsley wa taken down with fever. We put into a village and found it to be a large one. A few men came to the river bank. We spoke to them and one of them ran back to the village and told the news of foreigners near. In a few minutes a tall, broad-shouldered, bronze colored, well featured woman came walking slowly down the path accompanied by a number of other women. As I put forth my hand to greet her she told me her name was "Ngankabe."

I explained that there was a white man in the canoe sick. She at once without timidity stepped into the canoe, shook hands with Mr. Lapsley, and invited us to spend the night. We thanked her for her hospitable invitation, though we could not stay.

A Hostile Town.—Just as the sun was setting we put into a town to camp for the night. The villagers were up and under arms in a moment's notice. The war drum beat, the women screamed, and the whole town was in a terrible state of excitement. Guns, spears, bows and arrows were in the hands of the men, who were rushing in our direction. I stepped forward quickly and, picking up some beads and calico cloth, held them aloft and pleaded with the men not to shoot but let us land for the night. They brandished their spears, pointed their guns and called to us to leave at once or we would be killed.

With all my pleading and offering of presents they would have nothing to do with us. They only called in loud, excited voices, "Yaka! Yaka!" (Go away! Go away!) Seeing that our situation was perilous, I called to our men to pull on their paddles and directed them to cross the river for the other side.

Our boatmen were much excited and we feared for a while a fight between them and the villagers. We quieted our men, and urged them to paddle their very best. One shot was fired at us, but missed its aim.

The river was more than a mile broad and darkness was coming on fast, so we landed on a sand bank. We got up the tent and Mr. Lapsley was carefully moved into his bed. A fearful Congo storm swept down upon us that night and it was with great difficulty that we kept the tent and canoe from being blown away. Mr. Lapsley had taken a good dose of calomel and jalap and by midnight he was very much better.

All night we could hear the restless, excited natives on the other side of the river. Early next morning we secured our hippo which had been shot the night of our landing. We saw natives astride of their houses calling out in loud voices. Soon a big canoe pulled out from their side of the river filled with men. Another canoe followed, and still another. I ran into the tent and told Mr. Lapsley that the natives who ran us away last night were coming. We were not sure what they intended, but to be on the safe side we thought to offer them a part of our hippo meat. Beckoning to them, though they were coming any way, and pointing to the tempting meat, I continued with uplifted hands and loud calls, and before we could realize it to be a fact they had landed their canoes on the sand bank and were equally excited in fussing and fighting over the gift.

In the afternoon Mr. Lapsley was better and we were able to continue our journey. For another week, day after day, we made our way up the great Kasai river. We had many experiences with elephant, hippopotami and buffalo, with natives hostile and friendly.

When about 200 miles from Stanley Pool we reached the Kwango river. Leaving the Kasai to the left, we turned into the Kwango. After an hour's pulling we came to a very large village. The people were timid and had their spears, bows and arrows. As we pulled slowly to the landing the people rushed back from the beach, some of them running behind their houses; but with our many smiles and the tricks of our monkey, "Tippotib," who was playing at the bow of the first canoe, the villagers were attracted and came nearer.

We landed, bought a fine bunch of sun perch, a basket of eggs, and had dinner. Later we withdrew to an island and camped for the night.

A Sight for a Mission Station Offered Us.—Early next morning the chief from Boleke and his daughter

Antinobe, accompanied by two canoes filled with people, came to see us. They brought us chickens, fish and a number of bunches of bananas and pineapples.

We in turn gave a present of brass wire, beads, cloth and salt. We explained to the chief that we were journeying to Kinkunji, hoping to see a good place on which to build houses and live. We further explained that our work was to teach the people about God.

Our friends seemed to get some idea of what our business was, for the old chief offered us land in his own town and said he would charge us nothing for it. He urged us strongly to live with them. The next day hundreds of people crowded the beach and waved us good-bye!

One of Our Men is Captured.—When we were about five miles from our last camp one of our canoes was swept by the strong current under a low-lying limb and our man Mumpuya was knocked overboard. He swam ashore and was caught by the natives in the jungle. Hearing his screams for help, our canoe was quickly ashore and we were out and to the rescue. Through the high grass and jungle we chased the natives, who seemed determined to carry him off. One of the natives raised a spear to throw, but we were too quick for him, and with Mumpuya we were soon again in our canoes.

Being so menaced by the natives following us, and growing more hostile as we journeyed, we had to cross to the other side of the river, and in one of the towns we had many things stolen from us during the night while we slept.

No Proper Place for a Mission Station.—Though we had traveled a great distance in the Kwango, we had not seen a really suitable place for a Mission Station. The country was too low and swampy, the villages small and far apart. They had no king, but were governed by small chiefs.

The Last Two of the Lost Fourteen.—As we rested for our mid-day lunch, two men, much emaciated and almost naked, crawled out of the high grass and called to us in the BaCongo dialect. We were amazed.

"Who are you?" we asked.

They explained that they had been lost, fourteen of them, from a steamer on the Kasai river.

"Where are the others?" we anxiously asked.

"They have been killed by the natives," was the timid reply.

There were these two men who had been wandering for weeks, eating roots and what fruits they could get, and sleeping in the grass and jungle dodging the dangerous BaDima natives. Happier persons could not be imagined as we told these two lost men to get into our canoes.

We recrossed the river, and in crossing encountered no less than a hundred hippopotami. They rushed savagely at our canoes from both sides and only by keeping up a continuous fire from our rifles to frighten them could we pass in safety.

The Impassable Rapids of Mwamba.—On we journeyed, day after day, till we reached the impassable Rapids of Mwamba. We spent two days looking around the country and palavering with the chiefs and people. Not finding a suitable place for a Mission Station, we began our return journey to Stanley Pool.

Descending the Kwilu.—Our natives were in the best of spirits, we had a good supply of dried buffalo and hippopotamus meat, bunches of bananas, plantains and pineapples. Our head man blew several blasts from his big ivory horn, the men sang, and plied their long paddles with vigor as they stood in rows on either side of the big canoes. We glided down the swift river like young steamers. Our first camping place was where the Kwilu emptied into the Kwango river. We shot a hippo and secured him at once as he fell in the shallow water. We next camped at the confluence of the Kwango with the Kasai river. As soon as we had pitched our tent, half-clad natives came around with bunches of fish to barter for salt, beads and brass wire.

We left our camping place at peep of day, entered the Kasai river, the largest tributary of the Congo, and pulled at full speed till 3 P. M. We stopped on an island for a hasty lunch and continued our journey, hoping to pass the hostile village of Musye at midnight while the warriors slept. We were fortunate in having but little wind, for storms on these rivers are so dangerous that steamers must seek for shelter and tie up near shore. We kept as near midstream as possible. All was quiet save the bellowing of a bull hippo near shore, or the trumpeting of an elephant on the plain. We had some misgivings in passing this big town, Musye, which had made an attack on us when we were on our up-river journey. Now and then we would tell our men to paddle quietly and keep the two canoes near together.

Cautiously Passing Musye.—Even with all our precautions a great voice called across the water from a sand bank near the town:

"Who passes?" (No one answered.)

"Who passes?" came to us again in angry tones.

We thought it the best policy to answer, so our head man, Makwala, answered: "Friends are passing, going down to Stanley Pool." Again all was quiet. When we were certain we had passed the five-mile long town Musye, our men strengthened their arms and our canoes fairly flew. Another camp brought us into the waters of the great Congo river. We crossed to the right bank and camped just above what is known as N'Ganches Point.

Lions on the Right Bank.—Our men informed us that there were lions in the neighborhood, so we gathered wood from the forest and kept a roaring fire all night. Consequently we had no visits from these intruders.

Stanley Pool.—In three more days we reached Stanley Pool. On this Kwango expedition we had met four new tribes, had seen the general topography of the country, knew its products in field, forest and river, and had useful information and experiences which would help us greatly in our next journey. We shot elephants, hippopotami, monkeys, eagles, ducks and other game, of which we ate much and bartered the rest to the natives.

God had blessed us with health and carried us safely through many dangers, for which we were more grateful than we could possibly express.

CHAPTER IV.

EIGHT HUNDRED MILES OF PERIL.

Turning Our Faces Toward the Kasai.—On March 17th we boarded a flat bottomed stern wheeler wood burning steamer, the *Florida*. After many blasts from her whistle, the crew, thirty native men, pushed her from the beach and climbed in over her sides.

Captain Galhier, a Belgian, had the steamer in charge. Mr. Sirex, a Dane, was the engineer. The engines, boilers, crew, wood, dining room, which was used as cabin, were all on the one lower deck. The upper deck being flat and weather boarded, was used for ropes, tools, chicken coop and a small pilot house. The *Florida* steamed very well and we tied up late that afternoon just outside of the Pool. The crew went ashore with their axes and from the forest they brought dead trees and cut them up in lengths of two feet to fire the engines with the next day. We were early to rest, lying on the benches on either side of the dining table.

March 18th.—Steamed to-day only seven hours. Tied up at the bank about a mile from a native village. The captain asked me to take the steamer's canoe and some of the men and drop down to the village and buy food for the crew, furnishing the money (brass wire the size of telegraph wire and cut in one-foot lengths). The village tried to catch us a few chickens, but did not succeed. However, we bought a bunch of plantains and a bunch of bananas—not enough for one meal for the crew. On returning to the steamer a tornado swept down upon us and we had great difficulty in saving ourselves and the canoe.

March 19th.—Last night's storm had driven the steamer hard and fast on the bank and it took two hours to float her again. The current was very strong all day and the wood, being wet, we made but little progress.

March 20th.—To-day just about noon a sudden storm broke upon us, and thunder and lightning and rain seemed to defy our reaching the beach. Big waves dashed over the *Florida's* deck and for a while we were in peril. The captain called to me and asked if he should stop, but I answered quickly, "No, captain, never; run her full speed on the shallow bank." By so doing she stuck fast in the sand while the men quickly (and I assisted them) made the chain fast around a near tree. When the storm had passed all hands, with the engines going full speed astern, pushed her off and we continued our journey, reaching the Kasai river in the afternoon. In our devotions that night we thanked the Lord for bringing us safely through another day of dangers.

March 21st.—The captain anticipated trouble. We could see the red waters of the Kasai running into the Congo like a mill race. All the tributaries of the Kasai valley run into the Kasai river, and just here at its mouth the Kasai is only about 150 yards across, with a great wall of rocks on either side. The fire bars of the boiler had been complained of by the engineer, who was unable to get up sufficient steam. The captain called me to the wheel house and asked that I take the wheel while he directed the course. I did so with pleasure. We steamed off, turned the nose of the steamer around the sharp point and into the strong current of the Kasai. The captain rang his bell for full speed. The *Florida* did her best, but the current was too strong. She quivered under the strain and was forced backward to the point from which she had started. Again we tried, but with the same result. The whirlpools and strong current seemed too much for the *Florida's* strength. Not a man on board spoke a word; all was still as death. The engineer was doing his best at firing. The captain again rang for full speed; we steamed for five hours, making only a half mile. While the steamer was under such an awful strain the rudder chain snapped and there we were in that awful current between a hill of stones and no rudder chain. I called out to the captain to keep her going, and then ran back to the stern of the boat, got hold of the iron bar which governs the rudder, and as the captain signalled to me with his hand, guided her safely to a sand spot just between two enormous boulders. The crew, as quick as a flash, were out with the anchor and made her fast. It was with thankful hearts to God that we stepped from the steamer, for we could have been so easily dashed against the stones and to the bottom of the river.

The steam was turned off and the captain and engineer held a parley of what was to be done. The engineer insisted on turning back for Stanley Pool, for, as he explained, the fire bars are all burned out and the steamer is very old. No, said the captain, it would not do to turn back. Let the boiler cool off and repair the fire bars tomorrow.

March 22nd, . Sunday.—All day the bellows and hammer have been going repairing the bent and broken fire bars. Mr. Lapsley and I spent the day in devotion and reading.

March 23rd.—Having finished the repairs, we made

an early start. All the packing cases which could be found were broken up and used for firing.

In five hours we had steamed about six miles. The river broadened and the current was not so strong. At 12 o'clock we put into a village, but the people were frightened and ran away, so we were unable to buy food for our crew. They had not had a square meal for three days. At 2 o'clock we were stopped by a storm. When the storm passed we hunted for buffalo. There were hundreds of tracks, but we returned empty-handed.

March 24th.—The captain asked if we would go in the canoe and shoot something for the men. We went, but found only two ducks. A native, who had also killed two ducks, pulled his canoe alongside of ours. We offered to buy them and when he passed them over he remarked that he knew our faces and that we had given him hippo meat when we camped in his town on our canoe journey, so he would have no pay. A kind act brings its reward, even in Central Africa.

We returned to the steamer with four ducks. The *Florida* continued her journey, making good speed the rest of the day.

March 25th.—We were detained at our moorings, as our men were so weak from hunger they could gather but little wood last night. They are in a pitiable condition and our food also is short. The captain said this evening that if he did not soon get food for his men he would go crazy.

March 26th.—At 10 o'clock we sighted a village. We steamed in and made fast and every man who could pull himself along went ashore and began trade for food. Chickens, ducks, hogs and a number of dogs were bought; also bunches of plantains and bananas. Though we stopped for hours it was hard to get the crew aboard again. After getting under way the captain found that he was five workmen short. So we had to stop again and send the canoe back for the men.

March 27th.—The steamer has been taking a rest to-day, as there was no wood to fire with. Mr. Lapsley has an additional patient on his hands. I took sick early this morning and Mr. Lapsley almost exhausted his medicine case, but the ipecac, dovers powders, quinine, calomel, jalap and a few other things brought me around.

March 28th.—The men have not eaten all their supply of hogs, dogs and fruit, so no one has cried for food to-day. We passed a village and attempted to land, but the natives brandished their spears and showed a bad temper, so we passed on.

March 29th, Sunday.—The steamer made a splendid run and we tied up early this afternoon. The beach was filled with natives selling dried hippo meat, fresh fish (Kasai salmon), chickens, eggs, native bread, bananas and pineapples, and wood is also plentiful. Captain tells us that tomorrow morning we pass through the famous and dangerous Swinburne Rapids.

March 30th.—We steamed off at peep of day. The captain, Mr. Lapsley (the ship's doctor) and I were on the bridge. In an hour's time we struck the swiftly running current. The ship staggered, creened to one side and tried it again. The many whirlpools shifted her from side to side. A number of times the water ran over the deck. The whole pass is a succession of stony reefs. There was a death like quietness with both crew and passengers. Only the heart throbs of the engine under her great strain and struggle could be heard. We breathed a sigh of relief when we looked back and saw the rapids running wild in the distance.

Along either bank there are miles of grassy plains, and we passed many villages, saw scores of men well armed with spears, bows and arrows. At 5 o'clock we dropped anchor near a small village. The people were a bit timid, the women and children taking refuge in the high grass, but the men continued their carving on a carcass of a great crocodile by the bank of the river. There was no cutting of wood for the steamer until our crew had their portion of crocodile cutlets.

March 31st.—Started off under full steam, but had not gone far when a storm swept down upon us, driving the steamer, which could not be controlled, right into the big trees along the bank and overhanging limbs broke the cabin in. The anchors were thrown over and held fast.

The waves drenched everybody and everything. The fierce lightning and sharp peals of thunder added fresh terror to the situation. When the storm had abated all hands helped in cutting away the limbs of the trees and repairing the battered cabin. The anchors were pulled up and we started off again, but we had not gone far when the contrary current drove us broadside into the bank and the trees, where we remained all night.

April 1st.—We made a good half day's run to-day, but were stopped at 1:30 on account of another heavy tropical storm.

April 2nd.—Last night our sleep was disturbed by a windstorm which threatened to break the chains and ropes of the anchors and put us adrift in the darkness without steam.

April 3rd.—To-day we stopped at a large village (about 500 inhabitants). The villagers were calm and received us kindly and our crew bought plenty of food.

The captain also bought bantam chickens. They seemed to be everywhere and the roosters crowed in the same language as an American fowl. In the afternoon the captain sighted hundreds of wild ducks on a large, sandy island, so we went ashore and shot a few. There were aigrettes flying around at close range, but we did not kill them.

The temperature at 4 P. M. stood 99 in the shade.

April 4th.—"Mount Pouggie" hove in sight early this morning. It is a high blue ridge, the only approach to a mountain in this region.

A village near the water refused to allow us to land. The captain didn't like it, so he blew a blast from the steamer's whistle and those warriors fell over each other getting out of the way.

We landed at another village and found the people to be cannibals. They were called "Basonga Meno," "Ba" for people, "songa" to file, and "meno," teeth— the "filed teeth people." Their teeth were all filed to a sharp point and their faces tattooed. They carried large spears and quivers of poisonous and steel arrows. Two tiny pieces of palm fibre cloth was all they wore. Many of them brought dogs which were bought at once by our boatmen for·food.

April 5th, Sunday.—The passage has been exceedingly difficult on account of the many sand banks. The steamer tied up early near a village where houses are different from others we have seen. They are made of bamboo about nine feet high. The door is reached by a ladder, which at night is pulled inside and the door shut so they are safe from leopards.

April 6th.—The wood being very wet, the engineer had much trouble in getting up steam this A. M. There are not many sand banks and the water is deep.   ·

We are sleeping near a village tonight where our crew can buy a good supply of food. The people here wear copper rings on their wrists and necks, so we believe there must be a copper mine somewhere back in the hills. Speaking of engagement rings, we have seen them weighing thirty pounds on the necks of the women.

April 7th.—We are camping in a creek, a tributary of the Kasai. The captain saw a storm coming in the distance and ran the steamer inside for protection.

April 8th.—The steamer ran into a number of snags, but without damage. We saw a very large herd of hippopotami sunning themselves on a sand bank, and also some very large crocodiles taking a sun bath with their mouths wide open.

April 9th.—One of the steamer's rudders was bent, and the steamer had to be lightened to be repaired. While waiting the natives brought goats and sheep to sell. The sheep have no wool on them. Some of them were bought and we had much noise from the bleating.

The country is thickly populated with towns from a hundred to three thousand inhabitants. The steamer stopped at many of the towns and bought wood for cowries and beads.

April 10th.—The rudders gave the captain much trouble to-day, and so we were compelled to camp on a small, grassy island in the middle of the river. There was no storm or perhaps we should have been blown to pieces.

April 11th.—We saw scores of large black monkeys leaping from tree to tree, and droves of parrots flying in the air as thick as blackbirds. Certainly thousands passed over us during the day.

April 12th.—On both banks of the river there is a dense forest of mahogany, ebony, iron wood, ever-

greens and palms. The natives came alongside our
steamer to-day and sold to the captain and crew about
fifty pounds of fresh fish and eels.

We have seen their seines a hundred feet long. They
drag for the fish between the sand banks. These fish
are dried for future use. The streams all abound
with splendid fish.

April 13th.—Myriads of mosquitoes kept our company last night. Hippopotami are scarce in this region,
but there are birds of all kinds—eagles, hawks, crows,
ducks, cranes, parrots, guinea fowl, quail, wild pigeons,
bats, and many birds of beautiful plumage. There
are plenty of elephant, buffalo and antelope; their tracks
and trails are all along the river bank. In this dense
and impenetrable forest there must be everything
imaginable.

April 14th.—At 12 to-day we cast anchor at a large
town and bought corn, plantains, bananas, beans,
peas, peanuts, dried monkey and fish.

April 15th.—By a special Providence we were delivered from a watery grave. Four different times the
steamer came near capsizing, caused by strong currents
and whirlpools. The Master has certainly been good
to us and has led us step by step safely.

April 16th.—We were delayed two hours by the ship's
anchor getting hung under the root of a tree fifteen feet
under water. Accompanied by a native, I went down
the chain and tried to get the anchor from under the
root, but it was not possible. One of the crew tried the
task alone, but lost his hold and was washed under the
steamer by the strong current; but we saved him as he
emerged exhausted from the stern of the steamer.

All hands at the steamer's windlass finally broke the
root. After three hours' steaming another strong cur-

rent caught the bow of the boat and turned her suddenly
around like a cork on the water. At 3 o'clock we an-
chored at a good landing where there were a number of
large native canoes moored under the trees. We knew
by this there was a village somewhere. The trail was
soon found and we went to the village a half mile away
into the jungle and found it to be large and walled in.

LUEBO RAPIDS IN THE LULUA RIVER.

The only entrance was by a small trap-door. We
crawled in and the steamer's crew followed. The chief,
"Makima," and the villagers received us kindly. The
town was clean, houses large and well built of bamboo
with two rooms to many of them. The people crowded
around Mr. Lapsley and asked to see his hands, and some
even ventured to examine them. They laughed heartily
and enjoyed themselves greatly. They had never seen
a white man before.

We bought plenty of food, some carved wooden cups, and then returned to the steamer.

April 17th.—Early this A. M. we left the Kasai river on our right and entered the Lulua river, which is narrow but deep.

The whole country was filled with palm trees; the hills and valleys and everywhere beautiful palms. There were numerous fishing traps along the bank, canoes skimming over the water, paddled by excited natives, getting out of the way of the big steamer, and plenty of natives and small towns on the right bank.

April 18th.—Last night the crew cut plenty of good, hard, dry wood, so we have high steam and the engine is hissing and puffing and the paddle wheel flying around at a great rate.

At noon we were all on the bridge with the captain to see the Luebo Rapids, the head of navigation and the end of our present journey.

Captain Galhier, on his departure, assured us that he would be back again in nine months. At this point we are 1,200 miles from the coast and 800 miles from the nearest doctor or drug store, but we were comforted by these words, "Lo, I am with you alway."

Chapter V.

Beginnings at Luebo.

Luebo, April 21st.—We pitched our tent in an open space between the forest on the north side of the Lulua river. The natives from a nearby town came swarming around to see the faces of the newcomers. They were well armed with bows, arrows and spears, but we put on our broadest and best smiles. A little excitement was raised and they all ran off to their town.

The darkness of the night added fresh fears. We could hear the howling of the jackals in the jungle and the hooting of the owls. Mr. Lapsley on his couch was sobbing audibly and so was I. So far from home, with thousands of people and yet alone, for not a word of their dialect could we speak. About 5 o'clock in the morning how our hearts were cheered when we heard the chickens in the town crowing. We laughed heartily and said, "Well, there is one language we understand, for the roosters crow in the same language as our American roosters."

Darkness Everywhere.—Not only were the natives' skin dark and their minds and hearts, but there was not a visible light in all the town. Mr. Lapsley tore off a strip from one of his garments, twisted it up into a thick string, placed it in an empty corned beef tin, filled the tin with native palm oil and lighted the taper, and so we had the first artificial light. When driver ants, scorpions or serpents disturb a native he reaches up and tears off a strip from his bamboo hut, sticks it between the smouldering chunks of wood and gets a light with which to chase the intruder.

The moon and star light is glorious and is looked forward to with great pleasure, and they seem to shine nowhere so brightly and beautifully as in "Darkest Africa."

Beginning to Learn the Language.—Of course, they had no written language. We went into the town and with pencil and book in hand pointed at objects. For instance, a goat, and they called out the name, "mbuxi"; pointing to a chicken, they in turn called out, "nsola"; to a person they called out "muntu." To get the plural we stood two people together, and they said "bantu." There was not a book in all the region. They had never seen a book, nor a piece of paper of any description.

Their First Book.—Mr. Lapsley had a large picture book, and the natives asked the loan of it. They excitedly crowded and jostled each other, eager to see and to touch it. .How strange it was. They turned and counted every leaf. And then had it upside down, for they saw as much in it upside down as they did right side up. It was all the same to them, for they had never seen a piece of paper of any description in their lives.

The First Day School in the Kasai Valley.—Mr. Lapsley smoothed off a small plot on the ground, for we had no slates or pencils, and with a sharpened stick he printed the alphabet; and he had the little boys and girls stand up and repeat the letters. They showed marked signs of intelligence, and soon mastered their A, B, C's.

The First Sabbath School.—The children, and some of the older people, too, came daily. We sat under a large palm tree and began in the most simple way possible to teach them about God and His great love for everybody in sending His son Jesus to save them·

What a strange story! How they looked at each other, touched each other, and laughed. One little girl, smiling and intensely interested, asked Mr. Lapsley, "Dina diyeye, kabidi?" (What is His name again?) And Mr. Lapsley, with a holy smile upon his lips, answered, "Jesus." "What is his Father's name?" followed quickly from the little inquisitor. Mr. Lapsley answered in their native tongue, "Here you call him Nzambi, the Great Spirit, and in our country we call Him God." "Where is His native village?" she anxiously asked. And Mr. Lapsley, delighted with her desire to know of Him, continued to explain.

A Strange Thing.—One morning as Mr. Lapsley's door blew open a native saw a strange sight. It was Mr. Lapsley on his knees by his couch with his face in his Bible praying. The native was anxious to know of me what it all meant, and so I had the pleasure of explaining to him that Mr. Lapsley, their friend, was talking to the Great King above, about them. The native was so pleased he ran back to the town and told it to the people. They had never heard of Jesus, never. And there was our Lord and Saviour Jesus Christ standing in their very midst, upon two bleeding feet, with two hands outstretched, bleeding, to press those millions to a broken heart, and they had never heard of him—never!

The First Ray of Light.—One day as Mr. Lapsley's face was shining with divine brightness, and as he was putting his whole soul into his sermon on God's love, to a large crowd of natives, a woman who was the leader of the town dances was so deeply touched that she arose, stretched forth her long arms and said distinctly and earnestly, "Why, Mr. Lapsley, if we had known

God loved us we would have been singing to Him."
Mr. Lapsley was so overcome that he could say but
little more. The Holy Spirit had made a deep impression on Malemba's heart, and she was almost yield-
ing.

The missionary of Jesus went back to his humble hut
with a heart overflowing with gratefulness and joy for
this first ray of divine light. He was restless and slept
but little. At midnight he was communing with his
Lord and said, "We thank Thee, our Heavenly Father,
for this the first evidence of Thy favor."

The people had given Mr. Lapsley the name "Ntomanjela," meaning a path-finder, for he had found his
way into their country, their homes, their language,
and into their hearts. Chiefs from distant towns came
down bringing presents of chickens, ducks, hogs, dogs,
goats and sheep and made friends with us.

A Girl Who Ate Her Mother.—One day one of Mr.
Lapsley's friends came up and told him that some cannibals had killed a woman and eaten her, and that this
woman had a little child who had also eaten of her
mother. Mr. Lapsley, the missionary, was horrified,
and inquired fully of the affair. The people told him
that the caravan would pass his way, and sure enough
just before dusk a line of tired slaves came marching
slowly by. Mr. Lapsley approached the head man,
the chief, and asked him to halt his people for a short
talk. The chief did not like to do so, but he stopped,
leaned on his gun and listened to hear what the strange
foreigner had to say. Mr. Lapsley gently asked why
they had killed and eaten one of the slaves.

The chief explained, as a matter of course, that the
woman's feet were swollen and she could walk no more,
so they only did as they always do with those who are

unable to march. Mr. Lapsley asked the chief to give
him the little six-year-old girl and the chief said he would
exchange the girl with him for a goat. Mr. Lapsley
said he would give some foreign cloth for her. The
chief agreed to turn over the little girl, "N'Tumba," to
Mr. Lapsley. So he called in a native woman to take
charge of her. This woman took the child down to the
river and washed her body and put some clothes on her.
N'Tumba, with other children in the village, was taught
the alphabet, attended daily services, and began to
show an intelligent interest in Sunday-school.

Buying Dwelling Houses.—Our tent was so small
and hot that we decided to buy two native bamboo
houses. They were built of poles, the sides of large
bamboo mats, roofed with long palm leaves sewn together and put on over-lapping very much as shingles.
These houses resemble very much tiny cottages eleven
feet square and nine feet high. The owner of the house
started with a very high price and we with a very low
bid. He came down and we advanced in our offer.
Soon we agreed on a price, a straw was picked up by the
owner and handed to us, he saying, "Chubika." The
straw was broken between our fingers, he spat on his
end of the straw and threw it over his shoulder and told
us to do the same with the end we had. The bargain
thereby was sealed. We counted out our native money,
cowrie shells, and paid for the house. And when we had
calculated it in American money, we found that we
had paid 50 cents for each house. Their houses are
built in sections and we soon had them taken down and
moved on our land and reconstructed.

We bought and planted palms, bananas and plantain
trees, and in front of our houses had the way nicely swept.
In the pleasant evening we would take our promenade

up and down this beautiful walk. We called it Pennsylvania avenue.

With the help of the natives we began to clear the forest, take up the stumps, and clean up generally. A chicken, parrot and monkey house was soon built, for there were many of these brought to us for sale, and they were all good for food.

We built a shed in the middle of the compound to be used for dining room, sitting room, doctor's office and divine service.

We made daily visits to the village, mingling with the people, learning their language and curious customs. They all wore their native cloth ranging from the waist to their knees. They were given to hearty laughter, joking, playing games and running races. Many of them cultivated the ground, raising manioc, peas, beans and tobacco, and others spent their time hunting and fishing. Every night there was a dance held in the big square in the center of the town. The noise from their tom-toms, ivory horns and singing filled the air until midnight.

Mr. Lapsley as a Doctor.—We found many of the people suffering from various diseases. Mr. Lapsley in visiting the towns always carried along his medicine case and dispensed medicines to the sick. To our surprise they took calomel, jalap, Livingstone rousers and compound cathartics without hesitating; and as for castor oil, they would lick the spoon and call for more. In two months the medicine case began to get low. Honestly, those people would swallow pills just as long as you would deal them out. Mr. Lapsley ingratiated himself into the hearts of the Bakete early.

A Grateful Girl. –Mr. Lapsley never charged the people for medical attention, but many of them showed their appreciation of his kindness by giving him little presents of peanuts, pineapples, bananas, sugar cane, etc.

But I never saw him more pleased than when a little laughing girl came stepping up and handed him a small string of sun perch. Mr. Lapsley had been her doctor when she was down with fever.

Moving into the Moonlight.—Before the chickens began to crow for dawn I was alarmed by a band of big, broad-headed, determined driver ants. They filled the cabin, the bed, the yard. There were millions. They were in my head, my eyes, my nose, and pulling at my toes. When I found it was not a dream, I didn't tarry long.

Mr. Lapsley and some of our native boys came with torches of fire to my rescue. They are the largest and the most ferocious ant we know anything about. In an incredibly short space of time they can kill any goat, chicken, duck, hog or dog on the place. In a few hours there is not a rat, mouse, snake, centipede, spider or scorpion in your house, as they are chased, killed and carried away. We built a fire and slept inside of the circle until day. We were told by the natives that when there are triplets born in a family it is considered very bad luck, so one of the babies is taken by the witch doctor and put into a deep hole where these ants live and the child is soon scented by them and eaten.

Big Black Ants.—We scraped the acquaintance of these soldier ants by being severely bitten and stung. They are near the size of a wasp and use both ends with splendid effect. They live deep down in the ground and come out of a smoothly cut hole, following each other single file and when they reach a damp spot in the forest and hear the white ants cutting away on the fallen leaves, the leader stops until all the soldiers have caught up. A circle is formed, a peculiar hissing is the order to raid, and down under the leaves they dart, and in a few minutes they come out with their pinchers filled with white ants. The line, without the least excitement, is again formed and they march back home stepping high with their prey.

White Ants.—These small ants have a blue head and a white, soft body and are everywhere in the ground and on the surface. They live by eating dead wood and leaves.

We got rid of the driver ants by keeping up a big fire in their cave for a week. We dug up the homes of the big black ants and they moved off. But there was no way possible to rid the place of the billions of white ants. They ate our dry goods boxes, our books, our trunks, our beds, shoes, hats and clothing. The natives make holes in the ground, entrapping the ants and use them for food.

Red Ants.—These ants are the size of yellow jackets and look like them, and are smart with their nippers and tails. They live in nests in trees like the yellow jacket. These ants are caught by the witch doctors, crushed, and the liquid squeezed into the eyes and nostrils of the people who suffer from sore eyes or bad colds, and the pulp is eaten by the patient.

Many months passed away while we were hunting, fishing, clearing the land, learning the language, teaching school and receiving visits from chiefs and people.

Idols and Images.—Indoors and out were numerous idols. Those inside guarded and cared for the occupants by night, and those outside kept their eyes on common enemies and saw that no one with an evil spirit entered the door.

Out of a limb of a tree these idols are carved into an

image having eyes, nose, mouth and hands. They are stuck in the ground and often from the nature of the tree sprout and grow. About 300 yards from the town where the paths part a very large idol seven or eight feet high is planted to break the power of any one entering the town with evil intent.

We saw a father and mother sitting under the eave of their house weeping over a very sick child. Soon the witch doctor appeared carrying a chicken in his arm, which he rubbed over the naked body of the child. He then went to one of these images and holding the chicken over the image broke the legs of the chicken, then its back, and wringing its neck off dropped the blood on the image, then on the child's face and body. The doctor left the chicken with instructions that the parents should eat it. In this way people are healed, as they believe, of their diseases.

Beautiful Brown Babies.—It was so strange to us that the babies were all born white, but in a couple of weeks they showed their substantial color.

When the baby is announced to the town by an attendant it is the signal for the many friends of the family to hurry with pots of cold water and drench baby and mother, half drowning them. There is much shouting and laughing, and many clay pots are broken during this first degree of annunciation. Palm oil is soon on hand and baby gets a greasy bath; a big break-down dance follows, and then food is served by the father to all the dancers.

In less than a week the baby's regular meal is supplemented by the mother's forcing with her fingers soft bananas and corn meal mush down the little one's throat. There is much kicking, struggling and strangling, but the mother assists baby by pouring in water and giving him a good shaking.

Fierce Feuds and Fights.—Time and time again our quiet was disturbed by the blowing of the ivory horns and the beating of their war tom-toms. On inquiry we found that one of their women had been stolen by people from another town. Our villagers were a quickly excited people and loved to fight. Men going only a few hundred yards from their town were always armed with a quiver of arrows, bow and spear. Often Mr. Lapsley was called to care for the wounded. The witch doctors would mark the wounded with different colors of paint, but the people had learned that Mr. Lapsley's medicine was more effective. We have seen our town in bloody conflict over a mere trifle.

Children of Nature.—They had two general seasons, the rainy and the dry, "muxihu, mvulu." Eight months comprised the rainy season, and four the dry. It did not rain incessantly, nor was it always dry, and it never rained every day, and seldom all day.

These seasons were divided into minor seasons, as windy, thunder, caterpillar, and cricket seasons. There was a period when the wind blew a breeze from the south, a time when the thunder rolled out its heaviest peals, a time when all natives gathered caterpillars to be dried for food, and a time for the coming of the delicious cricket. This cricket was four times as large as the American one and sang four times as loud and long. They live in the ground and come out at night to cut and eat grass, and the natives, with torches, capture and roast them for food.

We asked men for dates, or of their ages, and they could never tell us, but would mention an occurrence which took place when the stars fought together and fell from the elements, or when a certain king was killed.

The new moon was always looked forward to with great interest, for it foretold by the way it lay whether there was to be peace or war. A man going on a journey would say to his family that he would be back in so many moons, and to keep them accurately he would tie a knot at the appearance of each moon in a string which he wore around his neck. Their gardens and fields were planted on the light and dark of the moon, and children born under certain moons were fortunate or unfortunate.

It seemed to us there was no place in all the world where the moon shone so brightly and so beautifully as at Luebo, Central Africa.

The native week was divided up into three working days—"Miyiya, Nkela, and Ntoenkela." Every fourth day no one on account of the spirits went a long journey, hunted, fished or worked in his fields. The day was spent in sweeping around their houses, mending their nets, making mats, weaving cloth, and holding court. Court was held in the square of the town under a large shed. The people had their judges, jurors, lawyers and officers of the town, but no written laws, and all evil-doers were punished by fines. A man that was found guilty of murder was forced to hang himself.

There are many, many kinds of birds of the air, all known and called by name, and the food they eat, their mode of building nests, etc., were familiar to the people. They knew the customs and habits of the elephant, hippopotamus, buffalo, leopard, hyena, jackal, wild-cat, monkey, mouse, and every animal which roams the great forest and plain, from the thirty-foot boa-constrictor to a tiny tulu their names and nature were well known.

The little children could tell you the native names of all insects, such as caterpillars, crickets, cockroaches, grasshoppers, locusts, mantis, honey bees, bumble bees, wasps, hornets, yellow jackets, goliath beetles, stage beetles, ants, etc.

The many species of fish, eels and terrapins were on the end of their tongues, and these were all gathered and used for food. All the trees of the forest and plain, the flowers, fruits, nuts and berries were known and named. Roots which are good for all maladies were not only known to the medicine man, but the common people knew them also.

A Rain-Maker.—We saw a rain-maker in Bena Kasenga one day dressed up in leopard skins and his hair filled with hawk feathers, and in his hand were a buffalo tail and a sprig of a tree. This wild man claimed that he could bring rain, stop rain, quiet storms, and protect the people from lightning.

A Tribal Ordinance.—Any animal killed by man, beast or lightning shall not be eaten until its hair has been singed off by fire. By this process, as they explained, no communication can be sent to other animals of its final fate.

An Economical People.—The people were not wasteful! Every dead sheep, goat, hog, duck or chicken was eaten. Dead elephants have been found in the forest and over ripe, the pieces gotten together in baskets, carried to the town, cooked and eaten. We saw men put out rapidly in their canoes after a large dead floating fish.

With a Caravan Going South.—It was decided that I would take a two months' journey into the Bena Biomba country south of Luebo as far as Wissman Falls, so with a well equipped caravan we journeyed south, passing and sleeping in many villages, learning the dialect of a strange and strong people. A lake was discovered; also new streams, and some large game was killed. We made friends and treaties with chiefs, and told the people that at some future day we would send them teachers. We saw native cows for the first time. At one of the markets, which was held in the open, the people were cutting up a twenty-five-foot boa-constrictor into round roasts for sale. We saw many tusks of ivory, each of which would have brought from two to four hundred dollars in a European market. We bought chickens for one or two teaspoonfuls of small white or blue beads.

During the sixty-eight days' travel I found the country to be rolling land and alluvial soil thickly populated with good, industrious people. On my return to Luebo I was received warmly by Mr. Lapsley and the natives and a banquet followed the same night.

MENU.

Chicken Broth.

Stewed Fowl.   Roast Goat.   Manioc Chips.

Native Pumpkin.

Native Egg Plant.   Greens.

Bananas.   Peanuts.   Pineapple.   Plantains.

and

Tea, with Sugar.

Quaint Cooking.—During my absence Mr. Lapsley had improved on the cooking plant which had been formally installed under a palm tree. It consisted of a well built shed 10x10 covered with long palm leaves sewn together to keep out the sun and rain. Very solid ant mounds, the size and shape of a man's head, were used as spiders, and on three of these the boy cook, who was a mute, placed a pot or pan. To cook several things at once more ant mounds were installed. The cook always sat or kneeled on the dirt floor when preparing meals.

Coney Island.—Mr. Lapsley had found a nice new bathing spot a half mile above our old rocky landing. We would swim from the main land across to a large sand bank near the Luebo Rapids, and on the warm sand would enjoy hand over hand and leap frog and run races.

His Last Leap.—Ngoya, who was a good swimmer, left his clothing on the high bank and made a dive for the deep water. It was nothing out of the ordinary and but little attention was given to the performance. After a few moments, when Ngoya did not appear, we became alarmed. We watched and wished for the best, but there were only the distant ripples. With a canoe and a long bamboo pole we searched thoroughly. Could a crocodile have taken him off so quickly? Did his head strike a stone, or a snag? His clothing was carried to his wife, and there weeping and wailing soon followed. The unfortunate man was heard of no more.

Six Unseen Sights.—The Bakete, after having seen Mr. Lapsley's face and hands and making close examination of both, were anxious to see his feet. They begged and pleaded with him—men, women and children—to pull off his shoes and socks, his socks they called bags, that they might get one peep at least. To satisfy the crowd Mr. Lapsley exhibited his small, clean, white feet. The eyes of the people opened wide. They laughed, talked and pulled at each other, so pleased. Then they got on their knees and begun to handle them. Mr. Lapsley was ticklish under the bottoms of his feet and this caused him to join in with the admirers in a hearty laugh. This exhibition had to be repeated for the newcomers a number of times daily.

Matches were a wonderful fire producer. I have many times bought a chicken for a box of matches. It takes about two minutes to get fire out of two dried sticks in the native way, but with one stroke of a match on the box you have fire. They were a great novelty to the people.

The people were mightily afraid of guns. When you would raise your gun to shoot a passing eagle or hawk, they would scatter in all directions. Some were brave enough later on to examine our guns.

The people in standing around would see Mr. Lapsley writing. They would stretch their necks, come closer, watch the movement of his hand, see the little marks he would make. They inquired of him what he was doing, and he explained that he was putting down his thoughts. It was a wonderful thing to them that you could mark down your thoughts and they would stay there. Sometimes Mr. Lapsley would send me a note by one of the crowd, and when I would tell them what he had said, they were simply dumbfounded. To prove the truthfulness and usefulness of the "mukanda" (book), Mr. Lapsley would buy something in the town and send the owner of the article to me at the mission with a note to pay a hundred, or two hundred cowries, as the case might be. I would count out the cowrie shells and pay the debt. Well, it worked like a charm and then the people asked us to teach them how to write books.

The people when dressing their hair for a funeral, dance or wedding would pour water in a small clay pot and use this for a looking glass, so when we showed them our looking glass a foot long they went wild and offered goats, sheep, ducks, dogs, anything, if we would let them have that great "Lumunia" looking glass. And later on came the wonder of the world—a camera. A small black box with a real eye in the center, which could catch them, going or coming, walking or talking, fussing or fighting. With them it was an "nkissi," a spirit, a thing to be feared, and an evil eye, to fly from and hide.

Mr. Lapsley's gold watch always drew a crowd. With their mouths and eyes wide open they pushed and jostled each other to get a peep at the wonderful, mysterious, moving thing. When the lid flew open, how they would jump back and laugh! How carefully and wisely, as they turned their heads from side to side, they watched the little hand running at full speed. Then the back was opened and they saw a little wheel, a forward and backward movement. They then asked us to show them the little men down inside who do the pushing. Mr. Lapsley tried to explain, but it was useless, for they believed there were little people down inside somewhere to make the thing talk and walk.

With the Bakete even the sun didn't go of itself, but there were great big strong men who caught it as it descended, put it into a great canoe, and pulled it across the deep waters, and early every morning with their combined strength started it again on its journey.

Mr. Lapsley tried to explain to them that buttons, beads, looking glasses, guns, etc., were not thrown up on the shore by the great spirit in the foreign country, as they believed, but were really made by men.

A Traveling Minstrel—You may be surprised to know that in that most isolated part of the planet there were "traveling minstrels." They were the Baxilane tribe south of Luebo. There was a piano, a narrow table-like frame with strips of a special kind of wood laid across it and gourds of different sizes tied under these strips to produce different sounds. Two men with sticks like bass drumsticks performed on it. Then there were the big drum, the head made of goat's skin, and two small drums, with two small men beating them. Then came the little and big ivory horns.

None of the ninety members of the minstrel had to burn cork, for they were already and naturally made up when they came to town. They danced in the open square, forming a great circle. Such jumping, twisting and cake-walking! When any of the spectators were pleased with a dancer they went up and placed cowrie shells, Congo money, in their hands, and in this way they were paid.

CHAPTER VI.

MR. LAPSLEY'S LAST JOURNEY.

Mr. Lapsley Makes a Great Journey.—With tent, traveling bed and cooking utensils and a caravan of men, Mr. Lapsley began his march into a new country lying southeast of Luebo. His marches were from ten to thirty miles a day, according to the condition of the trail and the business he transacted with the chiefs and people en route.

The country traversed was mountainous and well wooded and watered. Day by day he marched, always pitching his tent in some friendly village. He found the people to be of the Lulua tribe and also found some Baluba living far away south. The people on the whole were docile and received him kindly, making him presents of goats, chickens, hogs and dogs.

The houses of the people were small, with conical-shaped roofs, the walls being made of large strips of bark from the trees and the roofs thatched with grass. The people were very scantily clad, many wearing only monkey skins.

In all the towns Mr. Lapsley told them the story of the cross. The people listened with marked attention. The story was a strange one to them. He was asked over and over by the Lulua people to make his home in their towns, sing to them, and teach them more about his God.

Far away south Mr. Lapsley met and made friends with a big chief, who gave him a present of two men, a little girl and a number of goats and sheep. Another chief gave him four hogs, some dogs and much food.

After Mr. Lapsley's extended trip far south and his careful and valuable investigation of people and country, he turned his face toward Luebo. All along the route natives who had fallen in love with him joined the caravan. In many cases men with their wives, children, goats, sheep and all their belongings followed him to Luebo.

How happy we were when a runner announced Mr. Lapsley's arrival. With the big ivory horn blowing and the drums beating, we ran down the banana walk to greet and welcome him home. He was tired, worn, and weary, and walked with a limp. He had been scorched by the sun, beaten by the rains, and torn by the thorns; his coat was in tatters, and his last pair of shoes worn into holes; but through all of this he had that heaven-born smile as he said, "Sheppard, how are you? I am glad to see you." Soon we had him seated in front of his cabin in a camp chair and a pan of cool fresh water for his tanned face and tired feet.

Our cook killed a goat and a feast of the very best we had followed. I could bear the burning sand with bare feet easier and safer than Mr. Lapsley could, so the last pair of shoes of the camp, though two sizes too large, were brought forth and put on his feet. But I could not refrain from withdrawing to the bushes nearby and there in the quiet I thought of the beautiful Southern home on the hillside in Anniston, Ala., of the clothing, food and comfort in that home, of the dear hearts of that home who so loved Mr. Lapsley, and I broke down in spirit and wept.

An African Fever.—Mr. Lapsley told me the evening of his arrival that every bone in his body ached, and that he felt as though he had been beaten with rods. A fever soon followed. I nursed him carefully and tenderly through it and he was much improved in color from the purges and quinine.

Tales of the Lulua Trail.—Mr. Lapsley entertained the villagers and me for hours with the story of his journeyings amongst the Lulua and Baluba tribes; of how he followed the trails, crossed the streams, saw and shot game, made friends with chiefs and people, preached the gospel to thousands of half-clad natives, and sang for them; and of how they hung upon his words and begged him to make his home in their towns. He told us about their idols, their fetiches, their superstitions, and how no one died a natural death, for in the minds of the people someone had bewitched the unfortunate; of how people were accused of witchcraft—men and women; of how they were tested by the witch doctors with a well loaded flint-lock gun, and if the gun did not fire when the trigger was pulled the person was not guilty, but if it did go off the accused was shot to death and therefore guilty.

Our First Colony.—The Lulua and Baluba who had followed Mr. Lapsley asked for a site on which to build their future town. He pointed out a large unoccupied section lying to our left, and the work of cutting down trees, digging up stumps and building houses commenced at once. In a short while others hearing a good report of Luebo and the missionaries, followed and settled around us. People of a far interior tribe, speaking a different dialect and calling themselves Bakuba, came also. They mentioned that their king ruled over all the tribes of the country. We were interested in their apparent superiority in physique, manners, dress and dialect. We asked to be allowed to accompany them to their country and king, but they said it was impossible, their king would never allow a foreigner to come into the interior. Mr. Lapsley's faith was so strong that he believed that the Lord would protect us and that we would enter.

Mr. Lapsley's Return to the Coast.—In these nine months we both had suffered a number of attacks of fever. The steamboat brought a letter from the Belgian Governor General calling Mr. Lapsley to come down to the capital on important business. The beach was crowded with natives to wave him good-bye. The stranger who had come to their land on a strange errand was now known and loved.

New Buildings Erected.—After some days I called the natives together and laid before them plans of two large new houses. They accepted and were soon off to the forest to bring the necessary material, and in less than two months the houses were completed. We built outhouses, fences, made gardens, and cut a large way through the forest, connecting mission and native village. The number in school and church attendance grew.

Now and then for a change we would go elephant or buffalo hunting. Monkeys were also plentiful in the forest just back of the garden, and food of a great variety was plentiful.

They Were Superstitious.—One midnight I was startled. The village was in an uproar. When I arrived they informed me that one of the men had died, and it was the custom for everybody to cry aloud, to wail, to make tears come anyhow. Any person not showing signs of grief is suspected, and after the funeral is accused of witchcraft and must drink poison as a test. If they vomit the poison they are by the witch doctors pronounced innocent, but if they do not vomit they die and therefore are guilty.

The twitching of the eye, the itching of the hand, the flying of a crow across one's house, the hooting of the owl in the jungle, a snake crossing one's trail, were all bad signs. When there was an obstruction in the trail they would never part, but follow each other on the same side, and if one stumped his toe and it bled freely, he would return, deferring his journey.

They called my attention one evening to the new moon. It stood very much on the point. They said, "There is going to be war, and we are going to sharpen our knives and spears and dip afresh our arrows in poison." I threw a clod of dirt at a man one day in fun. He was indignant, saying it meant very bad luck to him. Dreams are serious things and are always taken to the witch doctors for interpretation. One of our villagers was killed by an elephant. They believed an enemy sent the elephant. A leopard one day tore the face and shoulders of "Mimanini" fearfully. The witch doctors hunted down an innocent neighbor and accused him of sending the leopard.

No Deaths Were from Natural Causes.—Thunder, lightning and storm were sent by the Great Spirit "Nzambi," who hates them. Truly the souls of these people were enveloped in the blackness of an awful midnight.

The people were always asking of Mr. Lapsley's return to them. I comforted them by saying that he would be coming soon, for many moons had passed away, and I longed for his return. I had studied the new dialect of the Bakuba and had made every preparation for our expedition into the "Forbidden Land" of King Lukenga.

Sad News.—At 3 o'clock in the afternoon a native reported having sighted smoke in the sky down the river. "Chuck a chuck!" "Chuck a chuck!" (Steamboat! Steamboat!) cried the people, and their hands, legs and mouths got busy. "Ntomanjela waduadua, Ntomanjela waduadua!" (Mr. Lapsley is coming; Mr. Lapsley is coming.) Our hearts leaped for joy. I ran with the natives down to the river bank as the steamer hove in sight around the point. On she came steaming up the strong current. She touched shore and made fast. I looked on deck, but did not see Mr. Lapsley. The captain beckoned me to come on board. He handed me a letter and it told the tale—

"MATADI, CONGO INDEPENDENT STATE,
"W. C. AFRICA, *March 29, 1892.*

"Dear Bro. Sheppard:

"You will be surprised and grieved to know that your friend and comrade, Rev. S. N. Lapsley, while here at the coast was taken down with bilious hematuric fever, and the 26th of March died.

"Yours in haste,
"S. C. GORDON."

What a blow! I was shocked. My head became giddy. My knees smote together, I staggered from the deck, threw up my right hand to the hundreds of assembled natives and called out, "Ntomanjela wa kafua." (Mr. Lapsley is dead.) The weeping and wailing started at once. The news soon reached the village and there was wild excitement and grief. I sought a quiet spot in the forest to pour out my soul's great grief to Almighty God. I had nursed Mr. Lapsley in all his fevers, and he in turn had nursed me; and now the Master had separated us more than a thousand miles apart and had called him, the better prepared of the two, to himself.

The next day I wrote the following letter to his dear mother:

LUEBO, CONGO INDEPENDENT STATE,
W. C. AFRICA, *May 26, 1892.*

Dear Mrs. Lapsley:

I know that you have wondered why I have not written you, or why I was not the first to break to you the sad news, but as you may know we were a thousand miles apart, and at this point of the interior we get a steamer once, or perchance twice, a year.

About the 1st of January, your darling son was sick with a fever. In three days he was feeling much better. A steamer, the "Florida," came in just then. Mr. Lapsley and I both thought that a change for a month or so would be beneficial to him, and he also had some business with the governor about our land. He thought to accomplish this and look after the transport at the same time, so he secured passage and left January 6, 1892, for Stanley Pool.

That Wednesday morning, February 26, 1890, at the foot of W. 10th Street, New York, just a few moments before the "Adriatic" left for England, you placed your arms around your boy and gave him his last kisses and Godspeed till you should meet again, and turning to me remarked: "Sheppard, take care of Sam." We went at once into Mr. Lapsley's cabin and prayed that the good Master would comfort you and protect us. We held daily communion with God.

We spent a month in England, being together always. On board the steamer "African" we held daily private prayer, and would often mention and ask special blessings upon our parents whom we were leaving. We entered Africa and proceeded as we procured information. We had never been separated for any length of time since we left America. I can place my hand on my heart and look straight up to God and say conscientiously, "I have kept the charge you gave me; I have loved and cared for him as if he were my own brother." The last word of one of his sisters at the depot in Anniston was, "Sheppard, take care of Sam." It has not only been a duty of mine, but a pleasure. I have nursed and cared for him in all his sickness, and he has done the same for me. When I was sick his eyes knew no sleep. By my side he would sit and give me medicine.

On our canoe trip up the Kasai he was quite sick with hematuric fever. It was the rainy season and we were unduly exposed, so we camped for three days on a beautiful island near the Kwango. There was nothing we could get that was nourishing for him, and he remarked, "Oh! I wish my dear mother was here; she would know just what to do for me." Shortly after this trip we came to Luebo, and here we have labored as best we could in promoting the Lord's kingdom. Every day we would have prayer and talks with our people. Many nights when all was wrapped in sleep he would be walking up and down the walk, communing with God.

Yesterday, May 25th, when the steamer blew I at once ordered the people to sweep the walks and fix everything in order so that the station would present a nice appearance. I hurried to the river and the captain handed me a handful of mail. I hurried and opened a letter to get some news, and oh, how sad the news! I was struck dumb. He who left me a few months ago and said, "Good-bye, Sheppard; God bless you. I will return by the next steamer." Dead! Oh! is it possible? He, my comrade and co-worker, from whom I have not been separated these two years, now dead! It was sad, more than sad, when I broke the news, to hear the men, women and children weeping for him whom they loved. And to-day they have been crowding in and asking, "Is the news true?" The greatest weepers were the chief's family, whose son was Mr. Lapsley's personal boy.

My friend and brother has gone to be with Christ, and I shall see him no more. No more kneeling together in prayer! No more planning together future work! His work is done, and he is now blest with peaceful rest. Oh, that I could have nursed him! That I could have kneeled at his bedside and heard his last whispers of mother, home, and friends. This is my sorrow, that I was not by his side while he fell asleep. I know that your heart is breaking. I wish I could say a word to comfort you. Little did you know that his farewell was forever. But he shall be standing at the beautiful gate waiting for you. We shall all soon join him where farewells and adieus are unknown. We submit to the Master's will saying, "Not ours, but thine be done. What thou doest we know not now, but we shall know hereafter."

> "Sleep on, beloved, sleep and take thy rest;
> Lay down thy head upon thy Saviour's breast;
> We loved thee well, but Jesus loved thee best."

Humbly and obediently,
SHEPPARD.

CHAPTER VII.

INTO A FORBIDDEN COUNTRY.

Start for the Forbidden Land.—After some weeks had elapsed, I called our station natives together and laid plainly before them the perils of the journey. I told them, from the information which I had, that the trails which had been made by elephant, buffalo, antelope and Bakuba natives were many and they led over long, hot, sandy plains through deep dark forests, across streams without bridges, and through swamps infested with wild animals and poisonous serpents. And above all, the king had sent word throughout the land that we could not enter his country. Not a man's muscle moved. I said further, "Mr. Lapsley, your friend and mine, desired so much to journey into that land, and it was his purpose on his return to take this trip, but you have the sad news that he will journey no more with us." There was not a dissenting voice.

Had General Information.—I had picked up the Bakuba dialect from some of the king's traders and tax collectors who journeyed our way. I received from them much information of the general direction leading north toward the capital, the names of large towns on the way, of the market towns, the approximate distances apart, the streams to be crossed, and their names; of the leopard, buffalo and elephant zones, and the names of some of the chiefs of the market towns, etc.

We Hit the Sandy Trail.—Two days later, when all was in readiness, tents loaded, cooking utensils, a bag of money (cowrie shells), some salt, etc., we left Luebo, led by the Master's hand.

Kapunga Hears Her First Message.—My men knew from previous experience the right trail to take as far as the Bakete village, Bena Kapunga, which led us through Bena Kalamba. We camped for the evening and had a long talk with the old chief. I bought eggs, chickens, and some dried field rats for my people. As night came on, we gathered around the camp fire and sang one of the hymns, "We Are Marching to Zion,"

CANNIBAL DANCE IN THE CONGO.

translated by Mr. Lapsley, and gave a public gospel talk to hundreds of natives who hurriedly gathered when we began to sing.

A Dancing People.—The moon, large and beautifully red, rose in a little while. The townspeople brought out their tom-toms and ivory horns to sing and dance in the open.

My caravan was housed under a large shed, the village
court house, not far from my tent. From the drums,
the horns, the singing and the falling over the tent ropes
by passing natives and the many meddlesome goats
chewing on the tent, there was no sleeping till the first
"cock crow."

Seeking the Trail.—We spent three days in Bena
Kapunga before we could get our bearings for the next
big weekly market place. After much persuasion the
chief gave a man to show one of my men the trail to
Ngallicoco, a two days' journey. They together
journeyed to Ngallicoco and returned, bringing many
dozens of eggs and other food. My *own* man now knew
the trail, so the following day we packed up and were off.
We passed through a number of small villages, slept in
one, and in due time came to Ngallicoco. The chief
made us welcome to his town, but wanted to know at
once where we were journeying. I told him we were
looking through the country and visiting the many
villages, that I was not a bad man and I was a friend to
everybody, and that my business was to tell them of the
Great Spirit. The chief and his people seemed much
puzzled and sat around in groups quietly discussing
matters.

My First Blunder.—I was seated in front of my
tent and had picked up a handful of palm nuts and
amused myself by throwing them at a mark on a house
nearby. In a moment a man rushed out very much
excited. He gave two or three war whoops and the
villagers began to run in his direction. I became
alarmed and inquired of one of my men the trouble.
And he explained that the occupant of the house was
going to die, because I struck his house with a palm nut.
The man's "Life Medicine," or charm, had been made

by the witch doctor from palm nuts and no one dared strike his house with one. Immediately I went over to the excited crowd and explained my ignorance of the fact and promised to make reparation. It was accepted, so I begged the man's pardon and presented him with a chicken and we became friends again.

Live Idols.—I don't know of a place where I saw more idols than here at Ngallicoco. At the cross trails near the village were idols seven and eight feet high and alive, that is, the trees from which they were made were planted two feet in the ground and continued to grow. Four or more idols were planted at the door, an idol for the husband and wife, one for each child, and for each dog, and so on.

A New Story.—We held our prayer service and delivered the first message of love and light these people had ever heard. As night came on and the moon in her glory shone out, the big drums started and the people danced until the wee morning hours.

Born Hunters.—These people seemed to spend most of their time in hunting, from the numerous animals brought in—wild hogs, antelope, hyenas, wild cats, monkeys, bush rats, field rats, etc. The women busied themselves bringing in from the fields roots of cassava, bananas and greens. The streets were filled with little children.

The First Bakuba Village.—I met a young Bakuba who informed me that his name was Bope N'gola Minge. He invited me to make a visit to his town. I asked how far it was, and he told me the distance in the native way. I judged it was about three hours' march, fifteen miles. I was delighted, knowing that this man had full knowledge of King Lukenga's edict, and yet cordially invited me to his town. I left my caravan, taking with

CONGO CORN AND MILL.

me only one of my men. We made the trip up hill and down, through jungle and swamp, arriving in M'boma, the man's village, late in the afternoon. I was glad we arrived before sundown, because we have no twilight in the Kasai region, and the moon was falling back.

Real Indian Corn.—I met the chief, a fine young man, Hong N'joka, his name meaning an elephant the size of a mountain, though he was not quite so large. I was pleased with the villagers who came around in great numbers. The chief fed me on splendidly dried fish and corn pone. This was the first corn I had seen.

The Poisonous Cup.—The next morning we retraced our trail to Ngallicoco. There were so many meddlesome goats, sand flies and fleas we decided to return at once to M'boma. After two hours' marching and our hearts so glad with the prospects of getting safely into the first Bakuba town, we suddenly ran upon an excited crowd of people, most of them men armed with spears, bows and arrows. I called an immediate halt to my caravan. The armed force showed no signs of fight but rather to run away. Bope, my Bakuba friend, explained that they were giving a witch poison, and they never administered the deadly drug inside of their towns, but far out on the plain. On this information I started for the crowd, saluted them in their tongue, and to my horror as I drew near they were slowly driving a woman to whom they had given the poison. She ran about fifty yards, staggered, reeled, and fell with a thud. A shout went up from them all, "Naki! "Naki!" (Witch! Witch!) At once the witch doctor, a great, strong man, with eagle feathers in his hair, a leopard skin around his loins, leaped upon the woman's neck and crushed out the remaining life. Like a shot the men were off, and returned with loads of dry wood, placed the woman's body on the pile, poured on palm oil and stuck a torch to the heap.

My Friend Explained.—My friend Bope explained that someone died in a nearby village and they believed that the woman was the guilty party who had bewitched her. For if she had not been guilty, he said, the victim

would have vomited the poison. Well, I must acknowledge I walked into M'boma with rather weak knees.

Exchanging Presents.—The chief, Hong Njoka,
and I exchanged presents. He gave me a dozen chickens,
two large goats, one sheep, a big hamper of peanuts,
six full bunches of bananas and a warm welcome, while
I gave to him two pounds of salt, two yards of white
domestic, 500 cowrie shells, ten teaspoonfuls of blue
and white beads, a handful of tiny bells and a small
looking glass. The latter was the finest present of
them all.

A Flyless Country.—There was a constant gentle
breeze on the high plateau, not a mosquito anywhere,
and, strange to say, you seldom saw a house fly.

We Went Elephant Hunting.—The chief, who was
a great hunter and had skulls of every variety of animals
bleaching in the sun on stakes behind his house, invited
me to go with him to kill elephants. We had not gone
a half mile into the deep forest before we heard the
trumpeting of an elephant nearby. The chief beckoned
me to follow him, but suddenly there was a crash of
falling dead trees and the elephants, perhaps a hundred
or more, came like a cyclone thundering by. We
crouched behind a very large tree and let them go on
their stormy way rejoicing. When we had recovered
sufficiently from our fright we turned homeward.
Before reaching the village we shot a large black monkey
weighing about forty pounds. There was enough meat
for the chief, my men and myself, so we all enjoyed a
good supper.

They Stole My Pocketbook.—The next morning
I said to the chief that I would like to move on to the
next market place. So he replied, "Ngexa" (tomorrow).
That very night while all were quietly sleeping my half

load of money (cowrie shells) was stolen from my tent. Early in the morning I sent for the chief and told him of my loss, and I ventured more. I told him I would have my money or he would have trouble. The chief soon had his head men together under a large open shed and they deliberated for about three hours. When night came on, the chief came with the lost money and asked me not to make any trouble about it, for already the women and children were frightened. We were detained here at M'boma for twenty-nine days, but I had the pleasure of preaching, praying and singing for them in their tongue daily.

Down-Hearted and Depressed.—I longed for the trail which would lead toward King Lukenga. But no one, not even for money, would assist us. Wearied, tired, perplexed, really at an end, I took my camp stool and went outside of the village and into the quiet forest and sat down to muse and pray. Alone with God, no friend, no companion, no one. Alone! Alone! I cried like my heart would break. I returned to the village, walking almost like a drunken man. I paced up and down before my tent as a chained captive.

A Sound of Alarm.—"Oka!" "Oka!" rang out a very loud voice from one of the villagers, and I, too, stopped and listened, as did all the people, and peering down one of the many narrow trails a group of travelers were standing. They called to the villagers who they were, where they were from, and where they were going. And in a moment they disappeared down through a ravine. I asked the man nearest to me, "Who are they?" He whispered, "King Lukenga's trading men, on their way to the capital."

N'Goma, "The Lion-Hearted."—Not to excite the people, I withdrew gently and called N'goma, my head man. We went behind a house and I explained as rapidly and as impressively as possible of the men who had just passed and the direction they took. I asked, laying my hand on N'goma's bare back, "Is your heart strong?" He answered promptly and like a man of war, "It is strong." "Have you any fear in your heart?" N'goma looked me square in the eye and said, "I have no fear." "N'goma," said I, "follow those men's tracks over the soft sand, follow them! *follow them!* Make a cross mark in all of the off trails and don't come back. I charge you, N'goma, don't return, for I will follow your trail at once with the caravan."

N'goma Hits a Trail.—N'goma, with spear in hand, bare head, bare feet, bare back, save his loin cloth and his small pouch of cowrie shells, walked quietly out of the village, but when he struck the trail he was gone like an arrow shot from a bow. When we began to take down the tent and make preparation for moving, the villagers gathered around, touching each other and talking in a low voice.

The Villagers' Protest.—Hong N'joka, the chief, and Bope N'gola Minge, my friend, asked what I was going to do, and where I was going. I explained to them that I was going to visit some other towns. They protested, but to no effect, and stood wondering what to say or do while we moved quietly out and away.

They are Calmed by a Call.—Fortunately for us, there was no rain, and we followed N'goma's trail and signs for two days and came upon him in a village called Bixibing. As we marched in the people were frightened and ran to the bush, but I called to them in a loud voice in their tongue, "Ko-cinaka! Ko-cinaka!" (Be not afraid! Be not afraid!) They returned and settled down.

Welcomed by the Chief.—The chief, Kueta, came and saluted me, but his people remained aloof. We congratulated faithful N'goma, put up the tent, and made ourselves at home. N'goma explained that it was not possible to follow the king's men further, as they threatened his life and took to the forest.

Kueta Serves a Banquet.—In the afternoon Chief Kueta came, accompanied by some of the first men of the town, the judge, a lawyer, a witch doctor and the town's blacksmith, and presented me with about twenty bushels of corn, five chickens, a very large goat, a ham of a wild boar, a basket of sweet potatoes, a big basket of blackeyed peas, dried fish, bananas, plantains, pineapples, a small basket of field mushrooms, and five jugs of water.

Turn Back, Was the Word of the Chief.—The chief said, in his Bakuba tongue, "Here is something for you and your people to eat, and there is the big shed under which you and your people can sleep. Tell them they must not steal, nor interfere with the women and children, and ngexa (tomorrow) you must go back the way you have come."

Showed Myself Friendly.—In turn I thanked them and presented my usual present. I made myself free in the village, walked up this street and down the other, saluted this man and that woman, and tried to play with the little children, but they were shy. I bought six beautifully carved ebony drinking cups, then went to the blacksmith's shop, where there was a crowd of half-clad young men watching the smith make sparks fly. The smith was working on a hoe.

The People Work in Iron and Copper.—The people gathered most of their iron from the top barren hills or from sluggish streams in a deep ravine. It settles thickly on the surface of the water, and although red, it looks very much like moss. The native oven or small furnace was nearby where the ore is smelted into iron.

When we began to sing a large crowd settled down on the ground around us.

Steady, Conservative Farmers.—These people are different in appearance, physique and manner from the Bakete. They retire to their houses and couches early. They are strong, healthy farmers. We passed en route a very large corn field with stalks towering far above our heads. The villagers told me that they raised fifty and sixty bushels of corn to the acre, and two crops a year.

"Telling the Story Over Again."—The next morning early, before the people started for their fields or their traps, I called them together and had singing and prayer and a full, long talk on the fall of Adam and how Christ came to restore us to God's favor. The people heard every word I said and seemed so interested, but I fear they understood not, for they had never heard that kind of a story before.

Shooting Guinea Fowl.—I told the chief that I heard guinea fowl in the bushes, and I was going cut for them and not to be alarmed when he heard a big noise from my gun. The people had never seen or heard a gun.

In less than half an hour I returned with four guinea fowl. I presented Chief Kueta with two of them. He was frightened, but accepted them.

Making a Big Road.—I asked where the people brought their drinking water from, for they had no wells or springs. With two of my men we followed the narrow winding trail down through the forest to a small stream.

We returned and I suggested to the chief the advantages of a big, broad road to the water. He agreed. Calling twenty of my men and furnishing them with big working knives (matchets), we began cutting the underbrush and soon had a splendid open road all the way down nearly a half mile. We all had a refreshing bath in the cool stream. I knew that these people later on would see the advantages of an open road, for the heavy dew on the bushes and grass on chilly mornings was not pleasant, and, too, the many snakes could be seen before running upon them.

Jigger Picking.—Our feet were now so clean we all sat down on the bank and began to take out the little pests—the jiggers. They are just like a tiny flea and burrow under your toe nails and sometimes finger nails, lay eggs, and set up an irritation which causes you to fret and fuss. They give you fits and fevers. The toes of many natives are eaten off by them.

A Big Supper.—My men were pretty hungry after the hard day's work, so they put their cowrie shells (money) together and bought two dogs, killed them, and made enough stew well seasoned with palm oil and red pepper for the whole party.

Dogs Never Bark.—These dogs look like an ordinary cur, with but little hair on them, and they never bark or bite. I asked the people to explain why their dogs didn't bark. So they told me that once they did bark, but long ago the dogs and leopards had a big fight, the dogs whipped the leopards, and after that the leopards were very mad, so the mothers of the little dogs told them not to bark any more, and they hadn't barked since.

The natives tie wooden bells around their dogs to

know where they are. Every man knows the sound of his bell just as we would know the bark of our dog.

Another Warning.—Chief Kueta came to me early the third morning and said in gestures which bespoke earnestness and uneasiness, "Foreigner, you can't stop here." So I said to Kueta, "Well, why?" "It is against the word of our king," said he. "You must return the way you came," and he continued: "Not only will we be killed, but you and all your people."

I settled down in my chair to think seriously over matters.

The King's Fighting Men are Coming.—In less than two hours from the time of my warning the town was in an uproar. The king's trading men, who had threatened my man N'goma, had reached the capital and reported to King Lukenga having seen a foreigner on the road moving in his direction, and the king had sent down his specially picked fighting men to intercept, fight, and drive me back. I sat quietly in my seat in front of the tent and watched the people in their flight for the forest. My people began to gather around my chair, and the youngest of the caravan, N'susu, nestled on his knees very close to me. The king's people were now in full sight standing at attention near to the big shed. The leading man with his big spear called in a voice that rang through the village, "Now hear the words of King Lukenga: Because you have entertained a foreigner in your village, we have come to take you to the capital for trial."

Pleading for Chief Kueta.—I knew things were now serious, so rising from my seat I called to the head man to meet me half way. He paid no attention. I called a second time and walked up to him and began to plead for Chief Kueta. "I understand you are sent by your king to arrest these people." "It is the word of the king," said he. I continued, "The chief of this village is not guilty; he gave me warning and told me to go away, to return the way I had come, and I did not. It is my fault and not Kueta's."

They Heard.—The leader, leaning on his spear, replied, "You speak our language?" "I do," was my quick answer. "That is strange," said he. The leader and his men moved off some distance and talked between themselves. In a little while he came back to me saying, "I will return to the capital and report these things to the king."

My Message to the King.—I said to him, "Tell your king I am not a bad man; I do not steal nor kill; I have a message for him. Wait a moment," said I. Taking from one of my boxes a very large cowrie shell, near the size of one's fist, and holding it up, I said, "This we call the father of cowries; present it to the king as a token of friendship."

He Was the King's Son.—The men were soon off for the capital and we settled down, hoping and praying for the best. Kueta told me that the head man was King Lukenga's son and his name was N'Toinzide.

N'Toinzide stood more than six feet, of bronze color, blind in one eye, determined set lips, and seemed a man fearless of any foe—man or beast. The villagers told me many things of the king's son, both good and bad.

All Very Quiet.—The natives sat around on the ground in groups, and so did my own people, discussing the perplexing situation. I lost my appetite, my interest in hunting and the villagers, but that very depression and dejection brought me nearer to my Lord.

My Prayer.—O Master, thou who art everywhere and who hast all power, govern the heart of King

Lukenga, and may there be opened a road for thy gospel into the very heart of this dark land.

The Messengers Reach the Capital.—After some days the messengers reached the capital and reported to King Lukenga. "We saw the foreigner, he speaks our language, he knows all the trails of the country."

The King Calls His Council.—The king was astonished and called a council and laid the matter before them. They deliberated over the affair and finally told the king that they knew who I was.

Thought They Knew Me.—"The foreigner who is at Bixibing," said they, "who has come these long trails and who speaks our language is a Makuba, one of the early settlers who died, and whose spirit went to a foreign country and now he has returned."

The messengers hastened to return and accompany me to the capital.

I Heard the Message.—We had been longing and praying for days for the best. With the king's special envoy were many more men who had come through mere curiosity, as was their custom.

N'Toinzide stood in the center of the town and called with his loud voice saying who I was and giving briefly my history.

The villagers were indeed happy. They flocked around as the king's son drew near and extended their hands to me.

Denied the Superstition.—I arose from my chair and made these remarks: "I have heard distinctly all that you have said, but I am not a Makuba; I have never been here before."

They Knew Me Better Than I Knew Myself.—N'Toinzide insisted that they were right, and said that his father, the king, wanted me to come on at once to the capital. The people were mighty happy, Kueta, our host, the townspeople and my people, too. Their appetites came back, and so did mine.

With a hasty good-bye, "Gala hola," to Kueta, we were off.

A Beautiful Country.—The trail lay northeast by north with a gradual ascent. The country was well wooded and watered. No stones could be seen anywhere, and the soil was sandy. There were many extensive plains with magnificent palm trees, hundreds and thousands of them ranging from a foot high, which the elephants fed upon, to those fifty and sixty feet high. The forest everywhere was ever green. Trees blossomed and bloomed, sending out upon the gentle breeze their fragrance so acceptable to the traveler. Festoons of moss and running vines made the forest look like a beautifully painted theatre or an enormous swinging garden.

Muxihu is Drowning!—About five miles on our way we came to the deep, swift stream called the "Langala." A great tree had been cut down by the natives and they directed its fall across the stream and used it for a bridge. Muxihu was following in the middle of the caravan with his forty pound bag of cowrie shells tied on his head, a cord passing over the bag and tied under his chin. He lost his balance and fell. The heavy load took him full speed on his head to the bottom of the river and the caravan put up an awful scream for help. I had crossed, but ran back at once and stood. It seemed long before Muxihu appeared on the surface, then he struggled and sank again. Then I leaped from the bridge and swam in Muxihu's direction. As he arose again I had him by his two wrists and turned on my back and swam with him to the bank.

We were some distance down and some of my men
made their way through the thick undergrowth and
helped us to climb the bank. N'Goma and Mumpuya
could swim and dive, so they volunteered to dive for
the pocketbook, and in an hour they had it and we
started off again.

On the King's Highway.—We passed through two
villages and camped in the third. We had no trouble
in finding our way, nor was the way obstructed by the
villagers, and we had plenty of food and were in good
company.

En route from "Bixibing" we passed under many
"charms," in appearance like a very large hornet's nest.
These charms were suspended over the road by a string
tied to a tall bamboo pole and the charm was filled with
poisonous arrows, a warning to those who travel that
way. I was attracted by a large elephant tusk inverted
and driven firmly into the ground at the entrance of
the village court house, a big shed. The king's son
informed me that his father had visited the town and
had sat near that spot and the villagers had planted
the ivory there in honor and memory of his visit. On
this highway we saw many fresh buffalo tracks and also
tracks of deer. Through all the dense forest which
lies behind us we did not see a python, though we have
killed some on the plains.

Approaching the Capital.—On the last morning
our trail grew larger, the country more open, and the
ascent greater, until we stood upon an extensive plain
and had a beautiful view in every direction of all the
land as far as we could see.

The Capital in Sight.—We could see in the distance thousands and thousands of banana and palm
trees and our escort of Bakuba cried out, "Muxenge!

muxenge!" (meaning capital! capital!) Just before entering the great town we were halted at a small guard
post consisting of a few houses and some men who were
the king's watchmen.   They told me that on each of the
four entrances to the capital these sentries were sta-
tioned.   A man was dispatched to notify the king that
we were near.   In a short while the people came out
of the town to meet and greet us, hundreds of them, and
many little children, too.   Some of my caravan were
frightened and would run away, but I told them that
the oncoming crowd meant no harm.

N'Toinzide, the king's son, with spear in hand, took
the lead and the interested and excited crowd after
getting a peep at me fell in behind.

CHAPTER VIII.

AT LUKENGA'S CAPITAL.

Really a Great Town.—We marched down a broad,
clean street, lined on both sides by interested spectators
jostling, gesticulating, talking loud and laughing. The
young boys and girls struck up a song which sounded
to me like a band of sweet music and we all kept step by
it. N'Toinzide called a halt at a house which I presume
was 15x25 feet in size. You could enter the doors front
and back almost without stooping. The house was
made like all the others of bamboo and had two rooms.
There were a number of clay pots of various sizes for
cooking and six large gourds for water. My caravan
was comfortably housed. I did not put up my tent,
but took my seat in a reclining chair under a large palm
tree in front of my door. The crowd was immense, but
we had them to sit down on the ground so we could
get a breath of air.

The King Sends Greetings.—In the afternoon the
king sent greetings, and with it fourteen goats, six
sheep, a number of chickens, corn, pumpkins, large dried
fish, bushels of peanuts, bunches of bananas and plantains and a calabash of palm oil and other food.

The prime minister, N'Dola, who brought the greetings, mentioned that the king would see me next day;
also that the king's servants would take out of the village
all goats and chickens which I did not want for immediate
use.

No Animals in Town.—For, said N'Dola, no sheep,

goats, hogs, dogs, ducks or chickens are allowed in the king's town.

We Delivered Our Master's Message.—In the evening we started our song service and I delivered to them our King's message. The crowd was great. The order was good. I went to rest with the burden of these people upon my heart, and thanking God that He had led, protected and brought us through close places safely to the "Forbidden Land."

A Grand Affair.—Early in the morning we heard the blast of ivory horns calling the attention of the people to put on their best robes and be in readiness for the big parade. I saw there was great activity in the town, men and women hurrying to and fro. Soon two stalwart Bakuba with their red kilts on and feathers in their hats appeared before my house and announced their readiness to accompany me before King Lukenga.

They noticed an old brass button tied by a string around the neck of one of my men. Very politely they removed it, saying, "Only the king can wear brass or copper."

I was dressed in what had once been white linen. Coat, trousers, white canvas shoes and pith helmet. The officials on either side took me by the arm; we walked a block up the broad street, turned to the right and walked three blocks till we came to the big town square. Thousands of the villagers had already taken their position and were seated on the green grass. King Lukenga, his high officials and about 300 of his wives occupied the eastern section of the square. The players of stringed instruments and drummers were in the center, and as we appeared a great shout went up from the people. The king's servants ran and spread leopard skins along the ground leading to his majesty. I approached with some timidity. The king arose from his throne of ivory, stretched forth his hand and greeted me with these words, "Wyni" (You have come). I bowed low, clapped my hands in front of me, and answered, "Ndini, Nyimi" (I have come, king).

The Royal Dance.—As the drums beat and the harps played the king's sons entered the square and danced one after the other single handed, brandishing their big knives in the air. The king's great chair, or throne, was made of carved tusks of ivory, and his feet rested upon lion skins. I judged him to have been a little more than six feet high and with his crown, which was made of eagle feathers, he towered over all. The king's dress consisted of a red loin cloth, draped neatly about his waist in many folds. He wore a broad belt decorated with cowrie shells and beads. His armlets and anklets were made of polished cowrie shells reaching quite above the wrists and ankles. These decorations were beautifully white. His feet were painted with powdered camwood, resembling morocco boots. The king weighed about 200 pounds. He wore a pleasant smile. He looked to be eighty years old, but he was as active as a middle-aged man.

Trying to Clear the King's Mind.—When we had sat for an hour without further conversation, with only now and then a smile or a gentle laugh from him as the dancers amused and pleased him, I ventured to clear up the superstition which was between us. I leaned from my seat toward King Lukenga and getting his attention said briefly, "I understand, king, that your people believe me to be a Makuba who once lived here." The king replied with a smile, "N'Gaxa Mi" (It is true). "I want to acknowledge to you," said I, "that I am not a Makuba and I have never been here before." The king leaned over the arm of his great chair and said with satisfaction, "You don't know it, but you are 'Muana Mi'" (one of the family).

At the Close of the Day.—As the sun was setting in the west the king stood up, made a slight bow to his people and to me. His slaves were ready with his cowrie studded hammock to take him to his palace, for his feet must never touch the ground. His hammock was like the body of a buggy carried on two long poles upon the shoulders of many men. Through the shouts of the people I was accompanied back to my resting place. It was the most brilliant affair I had seen in Africa, but my! I was so glad when it was all over.

Singing Their King to Sleep.—Mumpuya, my cook, had prepared a splendid supper of chicken fried with palm oil, fried plantains and some tender roasting ears. I was both tired and hungry.

About 7 o'clock N'Toinzide, with a few of his friends, came to ask me to go with them to hear the king's wives sing him to sleep. In a little while we were there and stood quietly on the outside of the king's high enclosure. Their voices were musical and sweet, though I could only catch a word now and then. The words "Nyimi, Obetcaka" and "Ndimuka" (king, sleep and love) were very distinct. I was pleased that the people were so happy with their king. But the thought that brought me to tears was, would these people here and at Luebo, and the thousands between, ever gather in groups for singing to our King and adore him in family prayer?

Royalty Never Begs.—We returned to camp. N'Toinzide intimated if it was convenient and for me not to think he would beg, to give him a little foreign salt, some shells, beads and enough foreign cloth to put around his bare shoulders. I gave it with pleasure.

Before leaving he asked if I had another of those very large shells which I had sent his father. I found one.

Seeing the King's Palace.—Early the next morning I sent for N'Toinzide, and together we went to see

KING LUKENGA'S SPECIAL MEDICINE MEN.

the king. After reaching the first great enclosure, through which no one can see and none climb over, N'Toinzide gave several taps at a small wicker window high up. A curtain was drawn, a few words were whispered, and we walked on beyond until we came to a narrow entrance which had been opened by N'Toinzide's brother. We passed in and the door was shut and barred. We then passed through three more gates and waited. In a little while we were escorted through a double doorway, the side posts of which were beautifully carved.

AN OBSERVATION HOUSE OF KING LUKENGA.

An Interview With the King.—The king in ordinary costume was seated on a low stool and we were seated on a large exquisitely woven mat. The king greeted us with "Wyni" (You have come). We both leaned forward and clapping our hands twice repeated together, "Ndini" (We have come). During all the interview we clapped our hands after every sentence. If the king coughed we coughed, if he sneezed we sneezed. N'Toinzide's wife, Mbiwata, came in and sat with us, and so did the king's principal wife. Two slaves on their knees supported the king's back.

The Message.—After some preliminaries I told the king of my coming to his land with a splendid young white man whom the Bakete named N'Tomanjela— "a path finder." The king, anxious that I should know his vast possessions, interrupted me and said, "I heard of him, he was at Luebo, and those people down there are my subjects." He continued, "I have more people, the Bakumbuya, Basalele and Banginda are mine." Certainly I thanked him for the information and continued my story. "N'Tomanjela taught the little children how to mark on the ground what they were thinking in their heads. He taught them also about the Great Spirit, a great King. This King made everything—the trees, the rivers, the elephants, the ants, the sun, the moon and stars. *This King made everything.* I had the king's attention, so I continued: "This young man N'Tomanjela died and was buried and his spirit went back to the Great King. So I have come alone, and my real purpose here is to tell you of the Great King and have your full permission to tell about Him everywhere."

King Lukenga instead of asking questions about this King, as I really supposed he would do, leaned toward me, smiled, and said, "It is all right; you can tell it everywhere, but you can't leave the capital; you must stay here."

As we bowed out and away I thanked God that the king's heart was in His own hand, and that Mr. Lapsley's long desire had been accomplished.

Lukenga Old and Gray.—Lukenga, though old and gray-haired, was strong and normal in all of his faculties. I have seen here a hundred or more gray-headed men and women. A long-lived people.

The King's Living Room.—There were, I presume,

more than a hundred bamboo houses in the king's private compound for his wives, sons, daughters and slaves.

The wives are the ones who sing him to sleep and sing him up in the morning with appropriate songs.

The spacious living room is where the king holds his private council and palavers. The walls are covered with smoothly woven mats like thick wall paper. The rafters are held up by massive artistically carved pillars of mahogany. The clay floor was covered with mats, except a small space where a slow fire burns continuously.

Statues of Four Kings.—On an elevation were statues of four former kings. These statues were carved from ebony. They were highly prized and regarded as sacred.

One of them represented King Xamba Bulngunga. On his lap was something like a checker board. King Xamba's dearest amusement was in playing this native game.

Another had a blacksmith's anvil before him, for he loved the art of blacksmithing.

A great national dispute came between Xamba and another supposed heir to the throne. The different factions had fought and still the matter was not settled. So it was agreed that the two contestants make iron axes and proceed to the lake nearby and the one whose axe floated would be counted king. Xamba (so they said) made his axe out of wood and covered it with thin iron. On the day of the test before thousands of anxious disputers the axes with befitting ceremony were thrown into the lake. Xamba's axe floated and while the people shouted and fought, Xamba was borne on the shoulders of his strong men to the capital and crowned king of the Bakuba.

Bakuba Have No Individual Idol.—I have seen in no Bakuba village an idol. I mean a large piece of wood carved into an image to be dreaded or adored. The people wear charms around their necks, arms and ankles, and these have their local significance. A man has his charm on his wrist and before eating with his neighbor, drinking palm wine or smoking a borrowed pipe, he will lick this small charm to prevent any evil wish of his neighbor entering his stomach.

King Lukenga offers up a sacrifice of a goat or lamb on every new moon. The blood is sprinkled on a large idol in his own fetich house, in the presence of all his counselors. This sacrifice is for the healthfulness of all the king's country, for the crops, etc.

Replenishing My Pocketbook.—I sold a great number of small round looking glasses for one hundred shells each, and I could have sold a thousand or more. The women almost fought with each other for the possession of one. They had never seen themselves, only dimly in a creek or a small pot of water which served as a mirror. I also had some small white and blue beads and they, too, went quickly. A small bag of buttons, all shapes, sizes and colors, went in a hurry. The people tied them on their necks and ankles for ornaments.

As I sold to the people, they in turn brought articles for sale. Hoes, knives, rugs, mats, cloth, leopard teeth, wild boar teeth, live monkeys, parrots and other birds, eagle and aigrette feathers and things innumerable.

Happy, Happy Days.—I asked the king to have a large shed constructed before my door to protect the people from the intense heat, and in a week's time it was up. Every morning it was filled and overflowing with these traders and others. I preached the gospel to them. We would sing one or two hymns, have prayer, and then, as slowly and simply as possible I would tell the new and wonderful story of Jesus. The audience gave excellent attention, no moving, talking or laughing; only now and then a nudge or a significant glance at each other.

There were many, many questions which I had the pleasure of answering after each service. Poor people, without home, without father, without the Friend that sticketh closer than a brother.

The Origin of the Bakuba.—This tribe is called Bakuba by all the surrounding tribes, but their real name is "Buxongo." The king's private name is Kueta Mboykin. Their tribal marks are tattooed on their abdomens; also the two upper front teeth are extracted. The marks are put on by their mothers and the two front teeth are removed by the blacksmith.

From all the information I can gather, they migrated from the far north, crossed rivers and settled on the high table land. And with many expeditions fought and conquered the surrounding tribes.

Tradition says their first people, man and woman, were let down from the skies by a rope, from which they untied themselves and the rope was drawn up. These people are conservative and very proud. There are about 10,000 Bakuba in the capital, and it will take many journeys before we can estimate how many there are in the whole tribe. Their language is full, highly inflected and musical. They do not speak to the little ones in "baby language," but talk to them just the same as they do their elders.

The Return of Cibambi.—One morning Cibambi, one of my followers, called me aside privately and said, "I am dying." I said in surprise, "Dying! What do you mean, Cibambi?" "I mean long ago my tribe and these people fought. We killed some of them and now they have bewitched me." I talked and reasoned with him of how impossible such a thing could be, but it was useless. He spat upon the ground a number of

PRINCE MAXAMALINGE AND WIFE. (Son of the Lukenga of 1892.)

times and remarked, "See, I am spitting up my life." I saw at once it was a case of indigestion and I gave him some medicine, explaining that he would soon be well. But it was to no effect. He imagined that he was bewitched and no doubt would have pined away and died.

So I reluctantly granted his request, gave him money and a guide, a fowl and an old magazine as his transport papers and he started for home.

They Serenaded Us.—Many nights the Bakuba gathered around my house and with harps and voices made sweet music.

Their harps are something on the order of small crude mandolins, but they know how to play them. Around the home, in the field or on a journey they always whistle, hum or sing.

Another Royal Visitor.—Another son of the king came to visit me; his name was Maxamalinge. He was tall, weighed about 250, fine looking and had a splendid bearing. On the whole, very much dressed up and very dignified. A number of slaves accompanied him.

After a short talk he invited me to go with him to his house and have dinner. I was pleased, and together we walked through the town to his own private home. His house was surrounded by a number of private fences. The gates were closed behind us, and no one could see through; there were no cracks. His wife, Bulengunga, was busy cooking in an adjacent room—a real kitchen. There were three large rooms to his house, a reception room, bed room (in which is also kept his valuables—tusks of ivory, cam wood and big balls of copper and iron); and the kitchen. The houses of his slaves were just beyond the first fence.

Dinner was prepared for six, and we all sat down on mats and used our fingers eating from the various pots fresh fish, buffalo, greens and corn bread. The visitors as well as my host and hostess asked question after question, but it did not prevent me from enjoying a good, hot meal.

A Snake Charmer.—One of the servants sat at the

door and amused us by allowing a scorpion to crawl up and down his naked arm, and he also placed the scorpion under his arm pit. He did many tricks with the scorpion. He was also a snake charmer, and no snake, tarantula or scorpion would bite or sting him.

The King's Town.—The town was laid off east and west. The broad streets ran at right angles, and there were blocks just as in any town. Those in a block were always related in some way. Around each house is a court and a high fence made of heavy matting of palm leaves, and around each block there is also a high fence, so you enter these homes by the many gates. Each block has a chief called Mbambi, and he is responsible to King Lukenga for his block. When the king will deliver a message to the whole village or part of it, these chiefs are sent for and during the early evenings they ring their iron hand bells and call out in a loud voice the message in five minutes. The king desired of his own heart to give me peanuts for my people. I heard the messengers delivering the word and the next morning we had more peanuts than we could manage. In some of the yards there were trees with blooming flowers

No Lights in Town.—There was not a visible light anywhere in the whole town. "A chunk or two" is always kept smouldering in the center of the house on the clay floor. The housewife is always careful to have a handful of split dry bamboo near, and when anyone is stung by a scorpion or snake (which often happens) they start up a blaze and hunt for the intruder and medicine.

When there is neither moon nor stars it is truly a land of awful darkness, and is made more dismal by the yelping of the jackal on the plain. The moon shines nowhere more brightly and beautifully than on Lukenga's plain. And the beauty is enhanced by the thousands of majestic palms, and the singing of birds with voices like the mocking bird and the nightingale. I have sat in front of my house moonlight nights until 12 and 1 o'clock.

CHAPTER IX.

CUSTOMS IN LUKENGA'S LAND.

A Clean Village.—Every morning the "courts" and streets were swept. Men who had committed some offence were compelled to pull weeds and sweep the streets clean.

CONGO CLOTH.

There is a rule in all Bakuba villages that every man every day sweep before his own door. The only littered places I observed were at the four public entrances of the town where markets were held daily at 6 A. M.,

12 noon and 5 P. M.—sugar cane pulp, banana and plantain peelings, and peanut shells.

When the king's drum taps the signal about 9 P. M. at the conclusion of the sleep song there is not a sound again in the whole village.

An Honest People.—All the natives we have met in the Kasai are, on the whole, honest. Our private dwellings have never been locked day or night. Your pocketbook is a sack of cowries or salt tied at the mouth with a string. But now and then something happens that the rule may not become monotonous. N'susa, one of the boys of my caravan, misappropriated some cowries. I called him (in the presence of two witnesses) in question about the matter. He acknowledged removing the shells and innocently remarked, "You are the same as my father, and what is his is mine."

Very Superstitious.—Before a man starts on his journey the witch doctor blesses his charm—a palm nut, cola nut or a small antelope horn which is worn on the neck.

If two persons (and they never travel alone) come to an obstruction in the path (tree stump, etc.), they never part, but both pass on the same side. If either stump a toe and the blood runs out, they invariably turn back.

The itching of the hand, twitching of the eye, a crow flying across one's house, an owl hooting in the jungle, a snake crossing your trail, are all bad signs. The new moon was carefully watched whether it bore good or evil tidings. If the crescent lay with both points upward, this was a sign of peace. If it stood on the point, drums were beaten, horns blown, arrows dipped afresh in poison, for there was going to be blood shed.

A woman crying and holding her hands over a bruised eye came to my place asking for medicine. She said that early in the morning she and her husband had a quarrel, and he on his way to his cornfield was bitten by a snake. He returned home and beat her for it and said that she had sent the snake to bite him.

The capsizing of a canoe, the falling out of a palm tree, a hunter or traveler killed by elephant or leopard—these are caused by some enemy.

The Signal Leaf.—A woman under the treatment of her doctor and on her way to the creek for a jug of water carries in her mouth a leaf, which signifies to all that she must not be saluted. If she is cooking a meal and a neighbor comes in, she must not speak until she is through cooking and everything covered up. By speaking or talking someone can wish her evil and it enters the stomach by drinking or eating.

The Mother-in-Law.—A man never meets face to face his mother-in-law on the highway. The man steps off and hides or turns his face. He never sits near or eats with her at any time. He must always act shy. He honors her in this way.

No Eye-Witness.—A man accused of breaking the rule of honesty, if there is no eye-witness, is tested by putting his right hand three times deep down in a pot of scalding water, and if the skin begins to peel off, he is guilty; if it does not he is innocent.

Red Pepper Test.—The girl accused of misconduct is tested by the witch doctor putting a small piece of copper wire and a finger full of red pepper in her eye. If the copper wire falls out and the pepper does not burn her, she is innocent. If otherwise, she is guilty and must pay a fine.

The Poisonous Cup.—In the native mind no one dies an ordinary death: they have been bewitched by an enemy. The witch doctors are paid by the relatives of the deceased to hunt out the guilty one. Early in the morning with painted bodies, feathers in their hair, leopard skins on their bodies, big war knives in their hands, they proceed to run, leap, scream, ring iron bells up and down the streets, stopping and hooting at every door, until by some imaginary force they are held at someone's door. A great shout goes up from the chasers. The person is called out and accused. Of course, they declare their innocence, but they are taken to a shed called the witch's house. They remain there until the marketers come in from the country. In the meantime the accused is visited by relatives and friends, each expressing their regret and hoping the test will be passed.

The witch doctor cuts from a certain tree poisonous bark, pounds it up and mixes it with water and standing before the accused and the assembled crowd says, "If you are guilty you will die; if not guilty you will vomit the poison." The victim, knowing that he is innocent, willingly takes the bowl and proceeds to drink it all.

The Victim of the Cup.—The victim is told to walk and in about ten minutes the poison has its effect. If it acts as an emetic, a great shout of joy goes up from friends of the accused. The victim is allowed to be carried off to a secret place by friends and the excruciating heaving goes on for hours. If the victim, from the effects of the poison, staggers and falls, a shout goes up from enemies and the witch doctor leaps upon the neck of the fallen and crushes out the remainder of life. The body is then wrapped in a mat, taken far out on the plain and burned to ashes.

No One Lives Alone.—From the great Lukenga plateau as far as the eye can look you see villages dotted everywhere. You never find a family living alone isolated from a village. The people live together for mutual protection from enemies and animals. And usually everybody in a village is related in some near or distant way; but it does not keep them from fighting occasionally.

They Actually Court.—The Bakuba are monogamists. A young man sees a girl whom he likes; he has met her in his own town or at some other, or perhaps at a market place or a dance. He sends her tokens of love, bananas, plantains, peanuts, dried fish or grasshoppers. She in turn sends him similar presents.

They often meet, sit down on the green, laugh and talk together. I have seen the girls often blush and really put on airs. He asks her to have him, if she has no one else on her heart, and tells her that he wants no one to eat the crop that is in the field but her. The girl and the parents both agree.

They Really Marry.—On a set day when the market is in full blast, with hundreds of people from everywhere, the young man and girl, with their young friends, all dressed in their best robes, meet and march Indian file through the open market and receive congratulations from everybody.

The new bride and groom continue their march to the already prepared house of the young man. A feast of goat, sheep, monkey, chicken or fish, with plenty of palm wine is served and all is ended with a big dance.

Royalty Excepted.—The women of the king's household select their own husbands, and no man dare decline; and no man would ever be so rude or presumptious as to ask for the hand and heart of royalty.

Agreements Understood.—The husband knows that he must cut down the forest and assist in planting corn, millet, beans, peas, sweet potatoes and tobacco, hunt for game, bring the palm wine, palm nuts, make his wife's garments and repair the house. He is never to be out after 8 o'clock at night unless sitting up at a wake or taking part in a public town dance.

The young man before marriage sends a certain number of well woven mats and so many thousands of cowries to the parents of the girl as a dowry. If they cease to love and must part, even twenty rainy seasons from marriage, the dowry or its equivalent is returned to the man.

The wife is expected to shave and anoint the husband's body with palm oil, keep his toenails and fingernails manicured, bring water and wood, help in the field, cook his food, and take care of the children.

Love Medicine.—I have had many a man come and ask to buy love medicine. They think charms and medicine can do anything. I always told them, of course, that it was a matter of the girl's heart, and charms or medicines could not help out in their "love affairs."

They Love Large Families.—The Bakuba are morally a splendid people. I have asked a number of Bakuba what was their real ideal of life, and they invariably answered to have a big corn field, marry a good wife, and have many children.

Babies Born White.—We were astounded when we saw the first new-born baby. It was so very light. But in a few weeks the youngster rallied to his colors and we were assured that he would never change again.

Baby's Own House.—No baby is born in the regularly occupied house. A small house is built in the back yard and is surrounded by a fence of palm fronds. No one is admitted into the enclosure but a few women. The new youngster receives a bath of palm oil, then the notice is given and all the friends of the family with jugs of cold water vie with each other in giving mother and baby a shower bath. The drums beat and the dance in water and mud continues for hours.

Stuffing the Baby.—Until you get accustomed to it you would be horrified to see the mothers stuff their young babies. The mother nurses the baby just as any mother, but she doesn't think that sufficient. So she has by her side a small pot of soft corn pone and a pot of water or palm oil. She makes a large pill from the pone, dips it in the water or oil, and while the baby is lying on his back in her lap these pills are dropped in its mouth. Then the mother uses the forefinger to force the collection of pills down its throat. As the baby resists and kicks, water is poured down its throat to facilitate the process. If the baby strangles, the mother will shake him up and down a few times. When the feeding is over, he certainly looks "stuffed."

Baby Cuts Teeth.—When the baby is cutting teeth, the mother will tie a small gourd around its neck and insert the pointed end into its mouth, or use a piece of crude rubber.

When the child is seven or eight years old the two front teeth are knocked out by the blacksmith with a small pestle and punch. When a person gets sick he usually clinches his teeth. The two front teeth are knocked out so that the mother or witch doctor may insert a funnel and pour the medicine through.

Sick Folk.—I have never known any cases of measles or mumps and only a rare case of smallpox. Fever and pneumonia are the prevalent maladies. A person having fever lies out in the hot sun and sweats; with pneumonia they give a hot mixture of herbs. If a man or woman has a severe headache, they lie down before their door and the witch doctor walks up and down their backs, kneading them with his feet; or the "doctor" will have a hole like a grave dug in the ground, sticks laid across the top, a hot wood fire built below, then cover the fire with leaves and the patient laid across the sticks to smoke.

If they receive a cut, there are leaves which, when torn open, exudes a juice, and when applied will stop the bleeding. For headache a string is usually tied very tight around the forehead to give relief. But a permanent relief comes when the witch doctor cups the temples by placing on each a small gourd. This gourd with one end smoothly cut off draws the blood, and the patient is soon better. They cup any part of their bodies where there is pain.

As the Children Grow Up.—The Bakuba children have many games and but few toys. The girls have wooden dolls made by their fathers, and the boys make from bamboo bows and arrows. They shoot mice, lizards, grasshoppers, crickets, caterpillars, butterflie lightning bugs, etc.

They make mud pies and play market, and tie the legs of May and June bugs to see them fly around and buzz. They love to play housekeeping. They are also trained to do some work, as bringing wood, sweeping, or looking after the younger ones. There are no knives, forks or dishes to wash.

"Baby talk" is not used and the parents speak to the babies just as though they were speaking to grown-ups.

I have seen the children in the streets drawing with a pointed stick or their finger on the smooth sand men, leopards, monkeys, crocodiles, birds, snakes and other animals.

Acrobats.—The boys make a heap of clay and sod it, and with great speed run upon it and turn a somersault, lighting on their feet. A string of them together will play "leap frog," and hide and seek is great sport with them. In all these amusements they keep up a song.

Taught to Fight. —There is one thing you will certainly see them doing, both boys and girls, and that is beating their clinched fists into the hard clay just as hard as they can drive. A year later you will see them driving their knuckles against a log or a tree. In this way they become hardened and are used as a weapon in fights when they are grown. And, too, they can butt like a goat, so in their family fights they not only use their fists but their heads.

Children of Nature.—I spent hours at King Lukenga's and other villages playing with the little folks and trying to find out what they were thinking about. They had a name for the sun and moon, names for very brilliant and prominent stars and ordinary ones. The sun was the father of the heavens, the moon was his wife, and the stars were their children. The sun after going down was paddled around in a very large canoe on the great water by men who were more than human and started in the skies again. They knew that a year was divided into two general seasons, the rainy (eight moons), the dry (four moons); though even in the rainy season it doesn't rain every day and very seldom all day at any time; and in the dry season there is an occasional refreshing shower.

They knew the names of all the lakes, rivers and small streams. Roots that were good for medicine or to eat they knew. Flowers and ferns were called by name. The names of all the many varieties of trees, birds and animals they knew.

Kingly Counsel.— I was surprised to know from

Maxamalinge, the king's son, that every month the king had all the little children of the town before him and he in turn would talk to them, as a great and good father to his own children.

The king would have his servants give to each boy and girl a handful of peanuts. When they were out of the king's quarters there was many a scrap over these peanuts.

A Heavy Storm.—One night there blew a heavy storm, and the rain doctor was in it all. I could hear his whistle blowing and his loud voice calling to the storm to be still. Houses were unroofed, trees blown down, and fences wrecked. The next morning, men passing my place, said to me as they saluted, "A heavy storm last night." I answered, "Yes, a heavy storm." At midday two messengers from King Lukenga approached hurriedly and, kneeling, slapped their hands and said, "The king calls for you." "What does your king want?" I answered. They replied, "I don't know." I brushed my hair, put on my coat and started with the men. All along the street men were busy repairing their houses and fences. Some saluted and some did not. We approached the king's high fence, passed through a number of gates and into the king's presence. After a few preliminary remarks, he frowned and leaned forward, saying, "A heavy storm last night." I hastily answered, "Yes, king, a heavy storm, and I was frightened." He leaned back and said in a questionable tone, "You frightened?" Again I said, "Yes." He placed his hand under his chin, looking me square in the eye, and asked, "What caused that storm?" I told h m of the present rainy season, of storms down at Luebo, and naturally he would have them here. The king grew excited, made many gestures, and said in a loud voice, "My witch doctors saw your followers at our creek yesterday stirring up the water and that caused the storm which came down last night."

I was frightened, not knowing what would follow, so I answered (as I had often heard his own people) in a low, slow voice, "It is true, king, my people were at the creek, but they were washing my clothes and it could not cause a storm." I continued, "They used in washing what we call in the foreign country soap, and it caused the whiteness and foam on the water, but it is something innocent and cannot cause a storm."

The king leaned back and was again calm and remarked in a pleasant tone of voice, "Well, don't have your clothes washed any more."

They Had Never Heard a Gun.—I had now been at Lukenga's for a month. I had no calendar, but one of my natives was time-keeper, daily tying a knot in a string which was worn around his neck, and every seventh day we kept as the Sabbath. The people had seen my gun, but had never heard it. I ventured out one day to shoot some guinea fowls in the manioc fields, and snipe at a stream a half mile away. I succeeded in getting the game and returning. The next day King Lukenga sent for me and I was not so timid as before. I went, and he told me that farmers had come and complained that their crops of corn would die if I continued to shoot over their fields. I consented at once to shoot no more, explaining to the king that I would do nothing to offend them.

Trouble at a Funeral.—On the burial day of one of the villagers I saw a number of men coming down the street with a slave woman, whom they were having trouble forcing along. I stepped out and inquired the trouble, and they explained that the owner of the slave had died and they were going to bury her with the dead. I protested and ventured to rescue the woman and for about ten minutes the Bakuba, my people and I were tied up in a scramble. We were overpowered and on they went with their victim.

A Victim of Lightning.—It was reported after a storm that a woman had been struck by lightning. I went out to see her, knowing their custom of giving the poisonous cup to find out the person who had sent the lightning. I kept a close watch on the witch doctors, but I presume because I had preached so much against the wicked custom they did not have a public test. I fear though they went off secretly into the bushes or high grass and carried out their custom.

Under a Fatal Tree.—The report came one day from a market town far away that twenty persons had been shocked by lightning; some were killed. They took refuge under a tree from a heavy thunder storm. In their minds some enemy sent the storm.

Infected Money.—One day when out walking with some of the villagers I saw a few cowrie shells and began picking them up. My friends at once bade me put them down. They explained that some sick person had rubbed the cowrie on their own affected body and thrown them by the wayside, and the person picking them up would catch the disease and the affected one would get well.

Mr. Lapsley's Bible.—I was often with King Lukenga, always taking along Mr. Lapsley's Bible; it seemed easier for me to read, for there were marks in it from Genesis to Revelation. Some of the most choice and striking texts were underscored twice. The margins were filled with helpful suggestions.

The king always wanted to handle it and turn the

leaves. He had never, and neither had all his prede-
cessors, ever seen a book of any description, nor even a
scrap of paper. The book he was handling was the
sword of the spirit, the light of the world. That book,
as little as the king knew about it, was the "Lamp"
that should guide his people over the King's highway to
victory. Think of it, the first Bible in all the Kasai
region! All of my preaching to the king was in the way
of conversation. A number of times he had his wives
to assemble and in those cases I stood up. At several
of those meetings the king asked us to sing again "We
Are Marching to Zion, Beautiful Zion," etc. He did
not understand a word of it; the hymn was one of Mr.
Lapsley's translations in "Ke Keti," the preaching was
in Bakuba. We had no translated hymns in Bakuba.
Though they did not know the words, there was always
a serious and pleasant response.

Prying into the King's Customs.—My interfer-
ing with the men who were dragging the woman to her
death had been reported to Lukenga. He mentioned
it to me, saying, "The burying of the living with the dead
was far beyond the Bakete, who only bury goats with
their dead, and that is why we bury slaves; they serve
us here and then go with us on the journey to wait on
us there." I told the king in the strongest language I
could command that it was wrong without the least
shadow of justification. I tried to prove to him that
the poisonous cup was a very cruel and unjust practice
and there were no witches. And if they gave the poison
to anyone whose stomach was not easily moved they
would die. The king thought me very foolish, saying,
"If a person is innocent they can never die."

You Grow Indignant.—Seeing these awful customs
practiced by these people for ages makes you indignant

and depressed and also fills you with pity. Only by preaching God's word, having faith, patience and love will we eradicate the deep-rooted evil. Everything to them is run by chance, and there are evil spirits and witches everywhere.

Preaching in the Markets.—The people from the country and surrounding towns made the markets and they would always cease bartering for a short while as we held divine service. In this way the word spread and many people came long distances just to see and to hear.

Enlightened But in Darkness.—I was astounded to find a people in Central Africa so intelligent and yet so far from the truth. The kilt or gathered skirts worn by men and women are made from the palm fibre on their own hand looms. They all wear belts, many with beads and cowries tastefully worked in them. The men wear small conical-shaped hats, kept on to a tuft of hair by a long pin. Before a man takes his wife he must, bearing a present, proceed to King Lukenga, seek an audience, and have the king with his own hands place the hat on his head and run the pin through. No young man is permitted to wear a hat or marry a girl, it matters not how many days' journey he lives from the capital, until he sees the king and receives the blessing by the hat process.

Industries.—Blacksmiths were busy turning out axes, hoes, knives, spears and·razors. Others made mats, rugs, baskets, hats, cups, spoons and work boxes. Many made fishing seines and nets for catching animals in the chase.

Provision for the King.—Every man of every tribe in the king's country is taxed, and at stated times his representatives in every village collect the cowrie shells and report to the capital. One tusk of every elephant belongs to Lukenga. The skins of all leopards killed are collected and sent to the king. The fishermen who live near the river and small lakes send up a certain number of baskets of dried fish each year.

The hunters, Batwa people, send cured elephant, deer and monkey meat. The Baxabwa, who live on the great plains, at a certain season run down partridges, catch them alive, and send baskets full to the king. Lukenga has a large coop made of bamboo splits, and these birds are kept and fed for him and his family.

There is a time for the swarming of the red locust. They settle down over the country by the millions. These are gathered, scalded, and sent in baskets to the king. Caterpillars and grasshoppers are also delicacies fit for a king's table. Manioc, millet, corn, peas and peanuts were stored away in abundance at Lukenga's. Lukenga never slept hungry.

A Yearly Feast.—I had the pleasure of being at the king's at a yearly "get together." There were representatives from all of the king's villages throughout the land. They brought with them their musical instruments—drums, ivory horns, harps, etc. They brought their best clothes in long boxes made from bark.

When the houses were all filled they slept under large sheds. The streets were alive. You could hear them inquiring of friends of their relatives in distant towns. Everybody wore a big smile and was happy.

The women had been to the creek and rubbed the sides of their feet many, many times against a stone until there was a white stripe all the way around. They wore a copper ring on their big toe and walked pigeon-toed. The style was to make short steps with the big toe elevated. Garlands of ferns and flowers were on their heads and around their necks.

Daily, for two weeks they gathered in the big square, sitting in a great circle. The king and a few of his wives and sons sat on an elevated covered bamboo platform. The delegates from each town sat together with their chief in front. It was a beautiful sight! The master of ceremonies ran into the center, saluted the king with the royal mace, then laid it before the chief of a village.

The chief arose, made a few acrobatic movements, and from the center of the circle saluted the king and in a loud voice reported the health and prosperity of his town, told of the crops, the births and deaths, and then danced alone to the delight and amusement of all the people.

As the evening drew near the formal ceremonies broke up with the music playing, the people singing and everybody dancing.

As I walked unaccompanied from the crowd, I prayed that the day would soon come when these same lips would be singing another song, and there would be another report of births, health and growth of souls to another King.

Preparation for Death.—As soon as a boy is large enough to work, he is taught mat weaving. He must first make dozens of balls of string from the palm fibre. Then day by day he cuts the long bamboo poles into narrow splits. As he makes these splits they are tied up under his father's shed or under the eaves of his house from the dampness. When he has sufficient, he begins under instruction of his father, brother or a friend to weave his mats against the day of his burial.

When these very large mats are completed a corn cob

is stuck in each end to keep out the rats, they are then carefully rolled up in palm leaves to prevent their being soiled or smoked.

At death these mats are cut and securely fastened to a framework of strong bamboo in the shape of a large telescoping box, the coffin.

They Know Death.—I only mention one out of scores I have seen die. Nnyminym took to his bed. The witch doctors daily for a week gathered hands full of ashes from his neighbor's houses and rubbed on his stomach to counteract anything poisonous he had eaten in these homes. I visited the patient; also treated him, but Nnyminym grew weak and was moved from his bed to a mat on the dry ground under his shed in front of his door. I talked to him of having faith in God, but it was all so vague to him. Earlier than my usual time for calling, his wife sent for me, saying that Nnyminym was dead. Knowing their custom, I was not alarmed, but responded at once.

I found the family bathing him and putting on his burial clothes. I remarked, "You are hasty, I fear, in dressing him for burial," but the wife remarked with grief, "No, he will be dead soon." When they had fixed his hair, shaved his face and shoulders, anointed his body with palm oil and adjusted his legs back under him, they all sat in a semi-circle. His sister sat behind him holding his back. This was all done in a business-like way and in order and quietness.

Debtors to the Dead.—The wife asked in a calm, gentle tone, "What of your debts unknown ·to us?" Nnyminym answered calmly, "I have settled all my debts; but listen, I will tell you the names of those owing me," and without effort he called name after name as the wife broke small pieces of bamboo for each name.

These pieces of bamboo were kept and the debts collected after death.

Watching Death.—Now and then Nnyminym in his sitting attitude looked at his hands growing pale, watched the heaving of his breast, looked at his family and friends before him, drew a long breath as though very tired, and actually watched death steal his life away. As soon as his eyes were closed a scream went up from his wife, and the rest of his family joined in. A friend of the family took his sister's place of holding his back.

Then, as is the custom, all the town came with slow steps and moaning song, hands extended in the air or folded over the head to weep with the bereft. They all cried; those who really cannot cry squeeze out tears, anyway. They *must* cry.

In State.—The family friend made an elevated seat like a large armchair and removed Nnyminym from the low mat to the chair. They then placed on his head a new hat and an elephant tail in his hand; the latter to show his strength. While the men on the spot were busy making his oblong telescoping coffin, the people passed in review moaning. The whole night was spent in weeping and wailing.

The Funeral Dance.—The next day friends from neighboring villages joined with these and in their best clothes danced all day. These dances are to cheer up the bereaved family and to run away evil spirits.

Smooth Graves Eight Feet ·Deep.—The third day six men bore away to the graveyard just outside of the town Nnyminym's remains. The family and friends followed quietly behind. They gently lowered the coffin in the grave by hooks in long bamboo poles and covered it with banana leaves. The women with their hands put in the first clay entirely covering the leaves; then the men with hoes did the rest. A carved tusk of ivory was placed at his head. The wife and friends return to the town, and when the widow enters her gate she is not again to appear on the street for a year, remaining in solitude and with personal friends. She can eat only parched corn and peanuts.

Highly Civilized.—I grew very fond of the Bakuba and it was reciprocated. They were the finest looking race I had seen in Africa, dignified, graceful, courageous, honest, with an open, smiling countenance and really hospitable. Their knowledge of weaving, embroidering, wood carving and smelting was the highest in equatorial Africa.

CHAPTER X.

BACK TO LUEBO.

Denied a Leave of Absence.—I told King Lukenga that I loved him and his people, and that it was a real pleasure to live in his town, but that his subjects at Luebo were looking for my return, and we had started a school and other good work down there, and I desired to continue it. The king replied to my request that he wanted me to remain with him and not to return again to Luebo. After a number of appeals in succession my request was granted with the provision that I return to him in the near future.

Getting Ready to Move.—I mentioned to my followers that we would soon be returning to Luebo; they were glad and yet they were not. Their stay at Lukenga's had been exceedingly pleasant. They had eaten more hogs, dogs, goats and chickens than ever before, and were just as fat and greasy as could be.

A Beautiful Bird.—I was tempted time and again to ask the king for his beautiful gray parrot. It was always put by the servants on the outer high fence. Every morning when anyone approached the king's gate it would call out, "Batie by ne; Batie by ne!" (People are coming; people are coming). The bird was not only beautiful, but could talk fluently, sing, whistle and crow.

A Reluctant Farewell.—My men single file moved forward loaded down with Bakuba curios, cloth, rugs, masks, mats, hats, cups and plenty of food. The parting with King Lukenga was touching. He was king,

but he had a kindly heart, and I was removing from
those thousands the only light they had ever seen and ✓

A DWARF (BATWA).

was leaving them in their usual darkness. The king
furnished us with two guides and his royal mace for

safe conduct. Hundreds of men, women and children followed us out on the plain, waving, singing and shouting a farewell.

A Large Lake.—We returned by quite a different route. One hour's march from the capital we came to a large lake. Around it the growth of flowers and ferns was beautiful, and the air was fragrant from blooming trees. Tracks of elephants, buffalo and deer were everywhere. There were great mud holes where the elephants came to wallow and play.

One of the men in picking berries came across (as he thought and said) a bundle of snakes. I discharged my double-barrel shotgun at the horrid fold, but it was only one immense python. The men cut large hunks of it for food on the journey.

Our first day out we camped in a small village, Ibunch. Many of the villagers knew me, as they had sold me eggs at the capital.

Bartering with Batwa.—I saw a number of Batwa, a species of the dwarf family. They had baskets full of white ants, dried elephant meat and green corn. I bought a number of gray parrots and two live monkeys. These dwarfs live in the forest and spend their time in hunting. We were up and off very early next morning, made a heavy march, passed through many villages, making only a short stop for our guides to tell the villagers who we were.

Through a Dark Pass.—There was one forest that seemed interminable. It was damp and dark, and it took us four hours' hard marching on a narrow grassy trail to pass through. Elephants were so numerous that I fired my rifle at intervals to frighten them away. We camped for the night at Suembuya. The people gathered around in the evening to get a peep at us.

A Nimrod.—They pointed out one NiManini, who had just that day shot a leopard with his bow and arrow. The skin was beautiful.

There was a palm tree in the middle of the town, which had on its limbs certainly not less than 600 swinging birds' nests, and all the trees were alive with the song and chatter of these pretty yellow birds.

Taking Pills.—The people saw me taking pills and asked what they were. I told them that these made me strong for the journey. At once they begun to ask for them, so I dealt out according to the size of the person from one to five compound cathartics. They did not wait for water, but ate them, and seemed to enjoy them very much.

Our sleep at Suembuya was broken by the yelping jackals, and the people told us the next day that this village was in the zone of jackals, hyenas and leopards. In all the villages that we passed through we had singing and service.

Forward, March!—On we marched over plains, through forests, swamps and across streams. We passed through fields of corn and cassava three and four miles long.

Big Traders.—We pitched our tent for the night in Balong, and natives came from three nearby villages to barter with us. They brought dozens of large vampire bats, dried fish and eels, and stringed pods of red and black pepper.

The people were so pleased to have us and begged that we stay in their village for many days. They wanted to exchange parrots, monkeys and other things for cowries, beads and salt. I am certain I could have bought fifty tame red-tailed parrots, the most of them talkers, speaking the native tongue.

No (Tsetse) Flies.—In all my wanderings in this territory, by streams, through forests and over plains, I did not see a tsetse fly. How blessed these people are, being separated from the bearer of the deadly germ which causes so much sleeping sickness and death on the lower Congo.

Densely Populated.—I found on inquiring that in all directions there were thousands of Bakuba inhabitants. I wanted so much to visit them, and having authority from their king there would be no trouble.

On the edge of the town there was a very big depression in the earth. A villager explained it to be a driver ant den, in which the weaker of triplets was thrown. By this sacrifice the remaining two babies grew strong.

There were large trails leading out toward the valleys and hills, a sign of many people.

Transmitting Messages.—While at Suembuya I heard one of their great wooden drums going, beating out the dots and dashes, which were heard and understood by villagers widely separated. Messages are picked up and transmitted to any part of the country by this crude way.

Kept Late Hours.—Though in dangerous villages, because of prowling animals, we sat each night by a big camp fire with a crowd of interested and inquisitive natives until midnight. Men and women asked questions. "How do you get to the foreign country?" "What do you eat?" "What language do you speak?" "Talk some of it for us." As soon as I answered one question they had another ready. At some of my answers they laughed heartily. When I tried to tell them that we had a season of the year that it got so cold you could walk over streams without breaking through, and

that some of our houses were taller than a palm tree,
they incredulously shook their heads. They had never
felt a cold day or seen a high house. I told them how
we bought land and sometimes water, too.

Before I bade them good-night I showed them the
Bible and gave them "History" (His Story), the story
of Jesus. It was wonderful; they did not understand it.
But some day, through some missionary, the Holy
Spirit will make it plain.

LAPSLEY MEMORIAL CHURCH, IBANJE.

Think of it, thousands upon thousands of people
throughout this valley have never heard a word.

Ibanche.—The people of Ibanche heard of our coming and came far out into the jungle to meet us. Near
the town court house (a big open shed) I had my tent
stretched and lay down for a rest, for my body was tired
and my feet sore from the hard marches.

My rest was short, for the people fell over the tent
ropes, trying to get a peep inside. I had my dinner of
chicken fried with palm oil, boiled greens seasoned with
palm oil, and red pepper and corn pone greased over

with palm oil. Then I took a walk up and down the two streets, followed by scores of happy men, women and children. The houses, with a few exceptions, were not as large as those at King Lukenga's, but built on the same style. Most of them had small trees growing at each end and strong cords around the trees and fastened to the end of the houses to steady them in storms.

The Witches' House.—The witches' house was a small shed in the center of the town under which the condemned person sat until market day, when poison was publicly given. They told me that hundreds of persons had sat under the fetich covered shed. I asked if the accused were not afraid and often ran away. They were surprised at the inquiry and replied with emphasis, "No, never! They are mad because they have been accused and are anxious to drink the poison to prove their innocence." Poor, deluded people without God and the truth.

Many Villages.—I visited the villages of Bongomba and Boincala, which were nearby. I was told that there were many other villages across the creek, and Ibanj was a great market center for all this district.

Nearing Home.—The guides told me that before us lay six large Bakete towns, Bena Kabu Bena Nsangala, Bena Kabash, Bena Kapunga, Bena Kalamba, and Bena Kasenga; and after passing these we would be back at Luebo. There was but one stream lying between and one very large and dark forest through which we would pass.

Under the Palms.—I had been away from Luebo for a long time and was thinking of the little day school and daily Bible lesson under the palm tree at Luebo. Those few little children, started in the alphabet marked fresh every day in the sand by Mr. Lapsley are still there.

The first daily Bible class, those same little ones who daily sat on mats and eagerly and inquiringly looked into the missionary's face as he patiently and most earnestly gave them their first lessons of Jesus, are waiting still.

Bena Kabau.—After an hour's march across a plain we were overtaken in the bush by a heavy rain, which lasted forty minutes. But we marched on; in fact, there was nothing else to do but to keep going. When we reached Kabau we took the chickens out of the baskets and tied them by their legs and turned the parrots into the street, then stood up ourselves in the sun to dry. There were plenty of sheep and goats in Kabau. The sheep have no wool on them. The little children brought baskets full of berries resembling very much strawberries. Under the town shed there were a number of travelers, Zappo Zap (cannibals). They were from the Baluba country far south and traveling north with a caravan of slaves to sell in exchange for ivory, rubber, cam wood and goats.

No Corn.—I tried to get corn for my people and myself, but could not buy any. These people raise and eat cassava, a root resembling a long sweet potato. When it is dried, beaten into flour and boiled it resembles very much a big ball of putty, though it is their staple food—bread. Bits are pinched off with the fingers, worked with the hands into small balls and dipped into palm oil or gravy and swallowed without chewing.

Freaks of Nature.—I saw two Albinos, a large boy and a man. They had rough white skin and wooly hair and very peculiar pinkish-gray eyes. They seemed entirely out of place. It made a shiver run through you to look at them.

We had our song and preaching service early in the afternoon. They had never heard of Jesus—never!

Traveling Minstrel.—At 5 o'clock about 200 Bakete people from Bena Chitala came into the town. The

SHAVING WITH A CHISEL.

women carried on their heads long baskets, in which was stored their clean loin clothes, strings of beads, cowrie anklets and their husbands' dress-up costumes. The men had their spears, bows, arrows, ivory horns and drums of many sizes. A very large camp fire was built in the middle of the street and they danced until daylight.

Preparing for the Last Dash.—Early in the morning I borrowed a native razor. They are made by the blacksmith from steel and look very much like a thin chisel. You wet your face with clear water and by many painful downward strokes you "chisel" off your beard.

Threading Through the Forest.—After leaving Kabau we passed through two large villages with short stops. Our guides said, "Now we have a real forest." It took us three hours single file following the narrow winding trail to pass through. There were but few spots where the rays of the sun had ever touched. In the denseness of the forest we did not even hear the singing of a bird. Scarcely a word was spoken until we emerged into the bright sunlight.

A Town Moving.—We found one of the villages on our route (Bena Kalamba) moving. The witch doctors, the lawyers, and all the important men had decided that the village had become unhealthy. Notice had been given to the people months before, and on the set day each man and his family by taking his house apart in sections moved to a spot previously selected. In moving the location is the same in the new village as it was in the old. So it is no trouble for a visitor to find his friends in their new homes.

The whole town moves a mile away in a day, puts up houses and occupies them when the sun goes down. All Bakete villages move every ten years.

Dispatching a Messenger.—When four miles from Luebo I sent a runner to let our people know that we were coming. Our man, N'Goma, though loaded with good things from the king's country, struck a trot and soon disappeared.

On we marched across the hot plain. In the distance were familiar scenes of forest and hills beyond our Mission and the Lulua river. We were filled with joy and gladness. God had been mighty good to us.

A Hearty Welcome.—They are coming! They are coming! cried one of our men, and they struck up a native song, singing at the top of their voices. And away yonder was a crowd like a great cloud with palms moving in their hands. They, too, started a song as they vied in speed with one another over the plain. For half an hour we greeted one another. They shook our hands, caught us around the waist, and many expressed their joy by letting the tears flow.

The caravan was soon relieved of their loads, for our friends—men, women and children, bore them away.

No Place Like Home.—In a little while I was seated in a reclining chair on my broad, cool veranda.

Making My Report.—The next day I called all the people, Bakete and Baluba, together and briefly made a report of our wanderings in the "Forbidden Land" of King Lukenga.

CHAPTER XI.

HIS KINGDOM COMING IN CONGO.

A Retrospective View.—From the time Mr. Lapsley and I landed on the Congo five years elapsed before there was a convert.

Those were great days, getting acquainted with missionaries and methods.

The walk of 260 miles to Stanley Pool; the return trip and across on the north bank to Manyanga; journeying to Bolobo by the steamer Henry Reed; the Kwango and Kwilu expedition in the rainy season with two large canoes; the exceedingly difficult trip of thirty days by a small steamer up the Kasai to Luebo; learning the language by sounds and signs; making treaties with chiefs and tribes; our explorations over land south to Malanje, the region of the Lulua and the cannibal tribe Zappo Zap; adapting and adjusting ourselves to inferior environments; the imparting of His great and glorious message to these weak and warped minds by signs, language and life was a joy far more than we could possibly express.

Twenty-six years ago two young men of the Southern Presbyterian Church went to Africa as missionaries, landed at Luebo, Congo Belge, with tent, a few articles of clothing and food.

They found the natives confused with many family feuds and tribal fights. There was not a married couple (from the Christian standpoint) in all the land. They had never seen a book. Not a prayer had ever been offered or a hymn sung. The Sabbath day was not known. They had never heard the name of Jesus.

LUKUSA, LATER CALLED "DICK," THE FIRST CONVERT IN THE KASAI REGION, AND THE FIRST MEMBER OF THE LUEBO PRESBYTERIAN CHURCH, RECEIVED APRIL, 1895.

But God's word was not to return unto Him void, and in 1895 a young boy about twelve years old, whom we called "Dick," professed his faith in Christ. Then in quick succession followed six other boys. There was joy in the presence of the angels, and who rejoiced more than the sainted Mr. Lapsley?

The Present View.—There are 51 missionaries of Jesus, zealous and optimistic in the great work for Jesus; 457 native workers, 15,674 church members, 275 schools, 15,934 students, 3 theological schools, 160 ministers in training, 338 Sunday-schools, 32,775 scholars, and 938 native teachers.

CHILDREN OF THE PANTOPS HOME, LUEBO.

The harvest of precious souls this year was 2,672, and 20,000 gather at 6 o'clock every morning for prayer.

Wherever there is a mission station you can ask the Christians to repeat for you not only a verse, but whole passages of Scripture perfectly. The Lord's Prayer, the ten commandments and the shorter catechism they know by heart. They can ask and answer every question of the catechism without a single mistake. Dozens of hymns they know and sing without the book. There is scarcely a Christian family without the prayer altar. They also have in their homes, or in the bush, a hiding place for secret prayer. Every convert is a missionary to the unsaved. They are liberal and count it a pleasure to give a tenth part to Jesus. The Sabbath is beautifully observed, no fishing, hunting or traveling. The witch doctor's business is fast passing away, the people come to the missionaries for treatment.

Think of the Pantops home with more than a hundred girls in training for Christian work. Girls are trained in domestic science and sewing. Campfire Girls and Boy Scouts are supporting an evangelist. Native Christians are running the big cylinder press, turning out hundreds of school books, hymn books, catechisms and the Bible. The books are also bound by them and used by thousands who were once heathen.

The native evangelists throughout the country preach twice a day, and a new sermon every time. When the big bells at the Central Mission stations ring out their inviting peals you can see hundreds of natives with their wives and children, hymn book and Bible under their arms, wending their way to the house of God. They sit quiet without even a whisper and are undivided in their attention. They are there on the King's business. The hymn is announced by the missionary and quickly they turn to the number and join heartily in the singing. The head is bowed in solemn and devout prayer. The chapter is mentioned and the people (sometimes thousands) turn to the book and chapter and read alternately.

No tongue can tell the great work that God has wrought through the Southern Presbyterian Church for these people, who only yesterday were in darkness ✓ and death.

A Prospective View.—There are in this region, and they are yours, 1,810,000 souls. Thousands have never heard a word; thousands have never heard of a missionary; thousands have never seen a single ray and are begging for the full light of the gospel.

What a vast harvest field! By the sign of the cross and in His name we shall conquer.

Index

DATE DUE

	AUG 2 5 2003	
ILL # AUG 33 1908		
due		
NOV 1 1998		
DEC 0 2 1998		
DEC 2 9 1999		
JAN 1 2000		
APR 2001		
2001		.